The
LD Teacher's
IEP
Companion™

Goals, Strategies, and Activities for LD Students

Molly Lyle Brown

D1571619

LinguiSystems

LinguiSystems, Inc.
3100 4th Avenue
East Moline, IL 61244

1-800-PRO IDEA
1-800-776-4332

Content Area:	Student Management
Ages:	5 thru 18
Grades:	K-12

FAX: 1-800-577-4555
E-mail: service@linguisystems.com
Web: www.linguisystems.com
TDD: 1-800-933-8331
              (for those with hearing impairments)

Copyright © 1998 LinguiSystems, Inc.

All of our products are copyrighted to
protect the fine work of our authors.
Copying this entire book for any reason
is prohibited. You may, however, copy
the worksheets as needed for your own
use with students.

Any other reproduction or distribution
of these worksheets is not allowed,
including copying this book to use as
another primary source or "master" copy.

Printed in the U.S.A.
ISBN 0-7606-0168-2

About the Author

Sitting still — looking serious — taking life seriously. Does it sound like a recipe for classroom disaster? Definitely, it's the formula for teacher burnout.

Whether I'm planning with colleagues, touching base with parents, adapting curriculum, or handling the latest "kid" crisis, I am in constant motion. And that's exactly how I like it. Educating kids takes energy, passion and taking risks, and picking yourself up just like you want your kids to be able to do.

My "risks" have included teaching students with learning disabilities at Bettendorf High School in Bettendorf, Iowa, for ten years. The next four years, I taught English to "regular kids" at the same high school.

Next came a six-year stint at LinguiSystems where I wrote, edited, managed people, and even talked to customers! I also coauthored three books — *Literature in Bloom, Bookshelf Favorites - Blue,* and *Bookshelf Favorites - Green.*

I am currently an LD resource teacher at Clinton High School in Clinton, Iowa. I love collaborating with teachers in the regular classroom and also helping kids with transition issues.

In my spare time, I continue to raise my three daughters and a granddaughter, grow flower gardens, collect dolls, hang with my buddies, and pursue my latest risk — marathon running. I just completed my first marathon!

Dedications

I dedicate this book to my best buddy and colleague Renée Simmons for helping me "pick my spot" through marathon running and book writing! You are an awesome friend, teacher, and coach!

Thanks also to my dear Clinton buddies Linda and Dana for all your cheering and support. I'm looking forward to a forever of Fridays!

Illustrations: Margaret Warner
Cover design: Roberta Johnson
Page layout: Christine Buysse

Table of Contents

Introduction 5

Math 7
   Basic Math Concepts 8
   Numbers and Counting 10
   Addition 13
   Subtraction 16
   Multiplication 17
   Division 19
   Fractions and Decimals 22
   Money 25
   Time and Measurement 26
   Word Problems 30
   Real-life Situations 31
   Geometrical Shapes and Concepts 33

Reading 36
   Phonic and Word Recognition Skills 37
      Auditory Discrimination 37
      Auditory Memory 41
      Visual Memory and Discrimination 42
   Reading for Pleasure 46
   Reading Comprehension 48
   Content Area Reading 54
   Vocabulary 57

Writing 60
   Handwriting/Letter Formation 61
   Written Expression 63
   Writing Process 66
   Forms of Writing 67
   Word Processing 72
   Everyday Writing 73
   Capitalization and Punctuation 74
   Grammar 77
   Spelling 78

Literary Concepts 84
   Characterization 85
   Plot, Setting, Conflict 86
   Literary Techniques 89
   Figurative Language 92
   Forms of Literature 93
      Fiction 93
      Nonfiction 95

Attention Skills 97
   Concentration 98
   Quality of Work 99
   Task and Assignment Completion 100
   Eye Contact 102
   Listening 103
   Behavior and Interaction 104
   Memory 109
   Organization 110

Study and Organizational Skills 112
   Organizes and Locates Information 113
   Reads Textbooks Effectively 115
   Completes Assignments 116
   Takes Notes from Classroom Lessons . . 119
   Takes Notes from Written Material 121
   Studies for and Takes Tests 122

Classroom Behavior 124
   Follows Directions 125
   Interacts in Groups 126
      Participates in Play and
      Group Activities 126
      Is a Cooperative Group Member 127
      Accomplishes Work as
      Part of a Group 129
   Works Independently 131
   Accepts Responsibility for Behavior 134

Table of Contents, *continued*

Social Interaction and Communication. 138
   Uses Problem-solving Skills 139
   Shows Social Sensitivity. 141
   Acts with Social Maturity 143
   Handles Conflict. 147

Transition to the Real World 149
   Self-Advocacy 150
     Recognizes Academic and
       Personal Needs 150
     Seeks Accommodations 151
   Career Awareness 152
     Identifies Skills, Interests
       and Aptitudes 152
     Researches Post-secondary
       Options. 153
     Acquires Important
       Occupational Skills 154

Workplace Readiness. 155
   Looks for a Job 155
   Applies and Interviews for a Job 156
   Interacts Appropriately with
     Co-workers and Customers 157
   Practices Job-keeping Skills 159
Everyday Living Skills. 161
   Understands and Manages
     Money Well 161
   Finds Own Transportation 162
   Cares for Self and Home. 163

Accommodations in the
   Regular Classroom. 166

Bibliography 168

Introduction

The LD Teacher's IEP Companion is an easy-to-use professional resource filled with hundreds of IEP objectives and activities or strategies for meeting them. This resource will shorten the time you need to plan and write your students' IEPs, leaving you valuable time for actual teaching. It will also help you plan lessons for your own classroom or in collaboration with regular educators in meeting your students' needs.

The LD Teacher's IEP Companion includes nine sections of objectives in areas where most students with learning disabilities have needs:

- attention
- classroom behavior
- literary concepts
- math
- reading
- social interaction and communication
- study and organizational skills
- transition
- writing

Objectives cover a broad range of academic, social and behavioral skills appropriate for students as young as first grade to students heading off to college. The goals and objectives provided parallel the expectations of students within the regular classroom since the majority of our students today are served within the least restrictive environment of the regular classroom. In addition, a separate Transition section is provided to ensure that planning for our students' futures begins as early as ages 12 or 14, and that our students are well aware of their needs and their rights when they graduate.

Individual Objectives

Within each section of *The LD Teacher's IEP Companion*, you'll find major goals listed for the year. The Individual Objectives suggested to meet each goal are worded so you can adapt them to fit the way your district expects you to write them and/or to fit the individual needs of your students. For example, a yearly Transition goal is "to prepare for future needs." Within a subsection entitled Self-Advocacy, one IEP objective is:

"The student will be able to ask for accommodations."

For your purposes, you may need to add specific criteria related to that area and how success is to be measured. You may rewrite the objective to say:

"Jared will ask for accommodations 80% of the time for English class."

Wording the objective this way may be appropriate for a student who is acquiring greater independence by beginning to make his own arrangements for accommodations, but who is not yet skilled or comfortable enough to handle all of them.

     Copyright © 1998 LinguiSystems, Inc.

Classroom Activities

For each IEP objective listed, *The LD Teacher's IEP Companion* provides a classroom activity or strategy that can be used by either the LD teacher or the regular teacher in the classroom. Recommended activities and strategies have purposely been designed to be:

- multisensory
- mastery-oriented
- usable in a variety of situations
- reliant on inexpensive, easy-to-find materials

Accommodations

Equally as important as IEP objectives are the accommodations you arrange for students within the regular education classroom. To help you plan such accommodations as part of the IEP, a checklist of Environmental, Motivational, Organizational, and Instructional Strategies is provided on pages 166-167.

Though designed specifically for the student with learning disabilities, the objectives, activities, strategies, and accommodations are also appropriate in meeting the needs of many students served within the regular classroom, like students with:

- attention deficit disorder
- mild mental disabilities
- behavior disorders
- autism
- physical disabilities
- language disorders

You'll find *The LD Teacher's IEP Companion* valuable not only for creating individualized education plans, but also for facilitating collaborative planning and teaching among special and regular educators.

Molly

Math

April takes out her strategy card listing steps for converting unlike fractions into fractions with common denominators. She makes the conversion and then successfully adds the fractions. Does she really know how to add fractions, you wonder? Certainly, the strategy card is a "crutch," at least for a while. But it's also a tool that temporarily relieves April of the burden of memorization. As she applies the steps over and over to more fraction addition problems, eventually April will understand the process and know the steps on her own.

You probably have many students like April whose math skills lag far behind their peers' due to:

- slow processing

- memory problems

- difficulty with abstract concepts

- language problems that make it hard to understand math concepts

- visual-perceptual or visual-motor problems that complicate copying, lining up and computing answers

Through the following classroom activities using methods like manipulatives, games, color coding, calculators, computers, and real-life simulations, your students can meet objectives in the areas of:

- Basic Math Concepts
- Numbers and Counting
- Addition
- Subtraction
- Multiplication
- Division
- Fractions and Decimals
- Money
- Time and Measurement
- Word Problems
- Real-life Situations
- Geometrical Shapes and Concepts

Copyright © 1998 LinguiSystems, Inc.

Math

Yearly Goal: to develop and improve mathematics skills

Basic Math Concepts ....

Individual Objectives

1. The student will understand opposites relevant to math, like *before/after* and *few/many*.

2. The student will understand similar terms, like *same as/equal* and *all/every*.

3. The student will understand comparative terms, like *high/higher/highest* and *late/later/latest*.

4. The student will recognize the concepts of and signs for *greater than, less than* and *equal to*.

Classroom Activities

1. Stock your reading corner with literature books that teach and reinforce math language concepts. (A good resource is *Math and Literature, K-3* by Marilyn Burns.[1] It includes sample lesson plans and a bibliography of literature books to use.) As a theme, teach two math opposites a week. Have students make their own math concept pages to illustrate and put in a book.

2. Create interactive lessons with your students. For example, ask all students wearing black shoes to stand. Then, have every student wearing black shoes to stand. Or ask a student to give another student five books. Then, ask a student to give you the same or an equal number of books.

3. Begin any comparison activity with just two objects or two pictures, like one tall block and one taller block. Practice with a variety of concepts, like *longer/shorter* or *wider/narrower*, so students understand the *-er* ending as it's used for comparison. Then, expand to using three or more objects or pictures and use of the *-est* ending. Make sure the first object picked for each activity is the one against which all other objects are going to be compared.

4. Use magnetic numbers and small objects to show relationships between numbers. For example, place the number four and four objects on the left, and the number six and six objects on the right. Let students count objects in each group and decide if four is greater than or less than six.

[1] *Math and Literature, K-3.* Marilyn Burns. Math Solutions Publications, Sausalito, CA, 1992.

Copyright © 1998 LinguiSystems, Inc.

Individual Objectives

Classroom Activities

To further aid learning, insert a *less than* symbol made from a pipe cleaner between the number groups. Write each relationship using numbers and symbols on paper as students continue to manipulate objects and numbers.

5. The student will count to given number values.

5. With objects or pictures, students count and then circle the correct number of objects to match a given number.

6. The student will match a numeral to the correct number of objects.

6. Give students 10 like objects. When shown a numeral, have students count out the matching number of objects. Progress to pictures of object groups to strengthen students' visual memory for quantity.

7. The student will add one more to a set of objects.

7. On the chalkboard or overhead projector, draw a number of simple objects. Then, have a student volunteer draw one more similar object.

8. The student will order things as 1st, 2nd, 3rd (ordinal numbers).

8. Relate order to your classroom routine. On a chalkboard, draw and number a few simple pictures to represent your major daily activities as they occur from the beginning of the day.

Check the Calendar   Reading Time   Recess

Then, using the picture time line, ask students questions, such as "What do we do third each day? Look at the picture by number 3 to see."

9. The student will use correct order terminology, like *before, after, next, first, second.*

9. Bring in fun objects, like different colored plastic dinosaurs or zoo animals. Let pairs of students put the green dinosaur on 1, the blue dinosaur on 2, and so on, so pairs are working with like items. Then, ask students to do things like point to the dinosaur after the green one, or to call out the color of the first dinosaur.

    Copyright © 1998 LinguiSystems, Inc.

Numbers and Counting ....

Individual Objectives

1. The student will count and read numbers from 1 to 10.

2. The student will count forward and backward.

3. The student will identify missing numbers in a sequence.

4. The student will compare numbers using >, <, or =.

Classroom Activities

1. Using shoe box lids as trays, glue common objects to represent numbers inside the tray. For example, two could have two buttons, or four could include four large pieces of macaroni. Also, write the number on the tray. As students count, they can touch the objects. To practice order of numbers, place trays out of order and have students count and reorder them.

2. Either with chalk on a playground or marker on butcher paper, make a number sidewalk. On each sidewalk space, write a number corresponding to the size of numbers your students can handle. Then, give verbal instructions to "move forward to number 5" or "take two steps backward." As students move, have them count numbers aloud. Use the number sidewalk for concepts, like *more, less than, greater than*, as well as adding and subtracting operations.

3. Tailor the activity from the previous objective by using number cards on the spaces instead of writing the numbers. Use blank cards for the missing numbers. As students walk the number sidewalk, have them count to figure out the missing numbers and then write them in. Use the sidewalk to teach concepts, like odd and even numbers, too.

4. Provide manipulatives for grouping. Also, make *greater than, less than* and *equal to* signs out of sponges or cardboard for students to manipulate. In pairs, one student can make a group comparison the other student has to solve by choosing the correct sign. For example, if a student makes a group of four on the left and a group of two on the right, the other student could place the *greater than* sign between them. Show students how to write number sentences for their groups, too.

Copyright © 1998 LinguiSystems, Inc.

Numbers and Counting, *continued*

Individual Objectives	Classroom Activities
5. The student will count by twos.	5. Have students make a fairly large drawing of something that comes in twos, like a pair of shoes or two eyes. Then, make multiple copies of their drawings so they can arrange the sets of twos on a large table or the floor as they count. (A student learning to count by twos to twenty would need ten copies of his drawing.)
6. The student will recognize the difference between odd and even numbers.	6. Using small tokens or other similar objects, make even numbered groups of items. Show students how every object in the even groups can be paired evenly with another object. Next, show students how with odd numbers of objects, one item is left without a pair. Then, below the numbers on a large model of a number line, place groups of tokens to show the even and odd groupings.
7. The student will count from 1 to 100.	7. Start a hundreds collection in your room. Have students collect everyday things like pop tabs, stones or buttons. Place individual collections in jars or boxes. Periodically, have students take out and count the objects as the collections increase. Have students group items by tens or twos and so on to begin to see relationships between numbers and items.
8. The student will identify the place value of two- and three-digit numbers.	8. Students who can read two- and three-digit numbers correctly can usually read any size number as long as they can determine the place it's in. Group bundles of ten straws together to represent tens and a single straw for a one. As you make different groupings, say things like, "Two tens and four ones. That's twenty-four." On a chart divided into two columns labeled *Tens* and *Ones*, write the numbers in the correct places. Use other grouping materials for hundreds and expand the chart to include a *Hundreds* column.

Copyright © 1998 LinguiSystems, Inc.

Individual Objectives

9. The student will write words for numbers between one and ten thousand.

10. The student will read and write numbers (between 1-100, up to 1,000, up to 10,000).

11. The student will round a number.

12. The student will estimate the answer to a problem using any mathematical process.

Classroom Activities

9. As you teach new number concepts, introduce the written word along with the number so students learn the word to number correspondence. Later, have students apply the skill of writing words for numbers by writing checks. On an overhead projector, show students how to fill in a check, including the date, who the check is to, and their signature. Then, dictate some purchasing situations, giving students the information to fill in except the amount which they must write correctly.

10. Make a colored border on two-by-two inch white cards to represent different place values. Include a card for the thousands' comma, too. For example, ones could be blue, tens green and hundreds red. As you say a number, students choose the correct number card(s) and place them in the right order according to place value. Students should be able to notice that hundreds are bigger than tens and so on. Some students may need tens or hundreds box patterns (two or three open boxes in which to place cards) drawn on paper and correctly labeled to facilitate placing and reading the number.

11. Use a rule and a visual reminder to help students learn the rounding rule, "If the number on the right is five or more, change it to a zero and go up one on the left."

$$
\begin{array}{c|c}
+1 & 0 \\[4pt]
4 & \cancel{5} \\ \hline
5 & 0 \\[4pt]
L & R
\end{array}
$$

12. On a regular basis, provide real-life examples where all you need to do is estimate an answer, not compute it exactly. For example, have students project costs of a field trip to know how much money to bring or the page count in a book to know how long it will take to read.

Individual Objectives	**Classroom Activities**
13. The student will count by fives and tens.	13. Let students use nickels and dimes to represent fives and tens. Students can practice by counting out five nickels to make twenty-five and then add five fives to check the counting. At some point, students may even discover reciprocal relationships, such as ten fives (nickels) equals fifty, and five tens (dimes) also equals fifty.
14. The student will read and write decimals.	14. Make decimal point and individual number cards for each student. As you read a decimal, have the student arrange the cards to make the number while also saying what it is. Eventually, have students write the decimal numbers instead of using the cards.
15. The student will compare decimals using *greater than, less than* or *equal to*.	15. When students are given a series of decimals to compare, have them highlight with the same color the same decimal places in each number, like all tenths pink, hundredths yellow, and so on. This technique helps students realize that a longer decimal number doesn't mean a bigger number.
16. The student will round decimals.	16. Relate the decimal to money. Ask students what amount the decimal is closest to, such as .36 is almost .40 or 40 cents. Then, review the "rounding up if it's greater than 5" rule.

Addition

1. The student will understand the concept of addition and the + sign.	1. Write plus signs on small objects, like Popsicle® sticks, so students see the sign as they hear the language. Take one stick and add another saying, "One stick plus another stick makes two sticks." Build math language for addition by saying, "One stick plus one more stick equals two sticks."
2. The student will know different terms that signal addition, like *sum, total* and *in all*.	2. Have students solve a lot of verbal story problems. Ask frequent questions, like "How many students in all are buying lunch today?" and have students count out the answer, or "What was the total number of students absent for the week?"

Copyright © 1998 LinguiSystems, Inc.

Addition, *continued*

Individual Objectives	**Classroom Activities**
3. The student will understand doubling a number and related addition facts, like 5 + 5 = 10.	3. Use a dot die so students can visualize doubles. Have students roll the die and add the sums by writing number sentences. Let students earn points for correct answers and bonus points for doubles facts they recognize immediately without having to write a number sentence.
4. The student will add horizontally or vertically.	4. Compare solving a horizontal problem to reading from left to right. Then, solve the problem by having students say the larger number and then "count on" the smaller number. Then, work the same problem vertically using the same process to show that the arrangement of the problem doesn't affect its answer.
5. The student will learn addition facts to sums of 20.	5. Teach addition facts as families. For example, the ten family would include 1 + 9, 2 + 8, 3 + 7, and so on. Encourage students to notice patterns in family pairs, like when one number goes up, the other one goes down. When students begin adding two-digit numbers, show the advantage of using a vertical arrangement.
6. The student will add three one-digit numbers.	6. Have students bracket or circle in writing and then add the two numbers whose sum is most familiar to them. For example, in 5 + 7 + 5, students may automatically recognize 10 as the answer to 5 + 5. They can then add or count on with dots or their fingers the remaining number.
7. The student will do column addition.	7. Have your students turn a lined piece of paper sideways to create columns as they set up addition problems. Or have them use graph paper to facilitate lining up numbers.
8. The student will add two-digit numbers without regrouping.	8. Color code each column a different color to represent the tens and ones. Then, have students add each column. Have students read answers aloud by saying five tens and six ones as well as 56.

Copyright © 1998 LinguiSystems, Inc.

Addition, *continued*

<table>
<tr><th>Individual Objectives</th><th>Classroom Activities</th></tr>
<tr><td>9. The student will understand the concept of regrouping.</td><td>9. Divide a shoe box into ones and tens sections. Using small objects, have students first add several sets of small number groups that make less than nine. As they add, they should say sentences like, "Five ones plus two ones equals seven ones." Then, practice adding numbers that make over ten. Show how the ten objects go into the tens slot with anything left over going into the ones. Write number sentences and answers on paper at the same time.</td></tr>
<tr><td>10. The student will add two-digit numbers with regrouping.</td><td>10. Draw a line between the ones and tens columns. As students add and have to "carry," explain that the ten in an answer ten or larger has to be carried to the next column past the line and regrouped with the other tens.</td></tr>
<tr><td>11. The student will add three-digit numbers with or without regrouping.</td><td>11. Make and laminate strategy cards that illustrate how to add multi-digit numbers with or without regrouping. Color code each column to show what numbers belong in a column. When a number is regrouped to the next column, color code it to match the column it's coming from to visually show that it has been moved.</td></tr>
<tr><td>12. The student will learn mental addition techniques.</td><td>12. Frequently pose addition problems by writing them on the overhead projector or chalk-board. Have students recognize what they do know, like an addition double or two numbers that add up to ten, and add from there. Have them estimate reasonable answers before checking their computation.</td></tr>
<tr><td>13. The student will do mixed operations, like adding and subtracting.</td><td>13. Have students color highlight the operation signs so they remember what to do. Remind them to say the problem aloud before solving.</td></tr>
<tr><td>14. The student will add decimals.</td><td>14. Use graph paper or lined paper turned on its side to create columns. Have students line up the decimal in the same box or column and write the other numbers in their corresponding box or column.</td></tr>
</table>

Copyright © 1998 LinguiSystems, Inc.

Addition, *continued*

Individual Objectives	Classroom Activities
15. The student will add money amounts.	15. Use the same technique as adding decimals, but make sure students include the dollar sign. Before students actually add, have them estimate a reasonable answer based on rounding an amount to the nearest dollar. For example, if students are adding $1.75 (2) and $2.06 (2), a reasonable estimate would be something less than $4.00.

Subtraction

1. The student will understand the concept of subtraction and the − sign.	1. Construct a large subtraction sign from stiff cardboard. Make subtraction problems by grouping manipulatives and placing the subtraction sign between them. Then, take away by having students count aloud the number being subtracted from the larger number. Last, have students count aloud what is left to find the answer.
2. The student will know different terms that signal subtraction, like *difference, how many less than* and *take away*.	2. Use manipulatives like small objects to help students visualize subtraction. As you make a group less or take away items, express the process with a variety of terms and write the number problem on a card.
3. The student will know the subtraction facts from 1 − 1 to 18 − 9.	3. Play Bingo-like games to encourage memorization. Put just the answers on the Bingo card. As you read a subtraction problem, have students cover the right answer.
4. The student will subtract horizontally or vertically.	4. Set up subtraction problems with manipulatives vertically as well as horizontally. Let students take away group members as you read a problem to them. Write the corresponding vertical or horizontal number sentence.
5. The student will subtract two-digit numbers without regrouping.	5. Some students may find it easier to subtract starting from the left as they do when they read. Explain that when there is a big enough number to subtract from on top, it doesn't matter if you start from the right or the left. Work problems both ways to illustrate.

Subtraction, *continued*

Individual Objectives	**Classroom Activities**

6. The student will subtract two-digit numbers with regrouping.

6. Color code the top number one color and the bottom number a different color so students don't automatically subtract the smaller number from the larger number.

7. The student will subtract three-digit and larger-digit numbers with regrouping.

7. Have students circle in color the numbers they need to change as they borrow to solve the problem.

8. The student will estimate the difference between two numbers.

8. Provide students with a choice of answers when they're asked to subtract two numbers. Then, discuss why one answer is more reasonable than the other.

9. The student will subtract decimals.

9. Allow students to rewrite the problem as a simple subtraction problem like they're used to answering. Then, show them how to insert the decimal in the correct place.

10. The student will subtract money.

10. Set up problems so students can understand the place value of coins and bills within an amount. Use columns on graph paper or specially lined paper to designate dollars, dimes and pennies. Have students then read the problem and its answer aloud to check their reasoning. Eventually progress to amounts requiring students to borrow from a column. Count out real coins as needed to show the amount borrowed.

Dollars	Dimes	Pennies
2	.2	6
− 1	.0	4
$ 1	.2	2

Multiplication

1. The student will understand the concept of multiplication and the **x** sign.

1. Rubber band or tie items in two groups of four, for example. Next, count the items in each group and write an addition problem to express the total. Then, show students a "shortcut," meaning multiplication, that they can use to find a total amount.

Multiplication, *continued*

Individual Objectives	Classroom Activities

2. The student will use a multiplication table.

2. Have students make their own multiplication tables to use for memorization of facts. Talk about some patterns they may observe on the chart, like multiples of 5 ending in 5 or 0.

3. The student will know words that signal to multiply, like *times, product, a piece,* or *each.*

3. Create a variety of word problems using multiplication vocabulary. Have students circle or highlight color the multiplication words as well as the numbers that will be used to solve each problem.

4. The student will multiply two-, three- or four-digit numbers.

4. Have students write their problems on graph paper, writing one number per box to set up the problem. As students write their answers for multi-digit multiplication, show them how the answer to each column of numbers after the first one shifts a box to the left on the graph paper. Color code columns and answer rows if needed, too.

5. The student will multiply by tens and hundreds.

5. Make number cards for 1-25. Make an additional 10 card and a 100 card. Demonstrate how a zero is added to the original numbers (2 x 10 = 20) when it is multiplied by 10. Do two to three more problems. Then, hold up a number card for the first problem. Place the 10 card behind it so that the number now reads 20. Repeat for the other two problems, and then do examples using 100. Have student pairs continue to work the calculations and then check with the number cards.

6. The student will multiply decimals.

6. Use both visual and auditory reminders for correct placement of the decimal in an answer. On a poster of sample decimal problems, underline in color numbers to the right of the decimal in the problem and in the answer. Write the rule, "There should be the same amount of numbers to the right of the decimal in the answer as there are in the problem." Have students say the rule as they place decimals in their answers.

Multiplication, *continued*

Individual Objectives	**Classroom Activities**

7. The student will multiply money.

7. Use play money to work real-life multiplication problems, progressing from even amounts of money to coin and dollar combinations. For example, students may need to purchase five pairs of socks for a sports team at a cost of $3 per pair. Let students arrange five groups of three one-dollar bills and then count them out. Then, have students write out the problem using the decimal point and dollar sign.

8. The student will multiply fractions.

8. Initially color code separately the numerators and denominators to show the numbers to multiply. Later, to show students how to reduce fractions as they multiply, purposely set up problems in which they can cross divide and color code those numbers.

9. The student will multiply mixed numbers.

9. As you write the problems, put a multiplication sign between the whole number and the denominator and a plus sign between the whole number and the numer-ator to remind students how to convert mixed numbers to improper fractions.

$$3 \, {}^{+}_{\times}\frac{3}{4} \; \times \; 1 \, {}^{+}_{\times}\frac{1}{2} = \frac{15}{4} \times \frac{3}{2}$$

Division

1. The student will do simple division by separating and counting.

1. Use small objects that can be divided by traits, like color or shape. Ask students how many you started with. Then, divide the group by trait. For example, nine objects might be three yellow, three blue and three green objects. Have students count the objects in each group. Write division problems using ÷ as well as the bracket to introduce the division process.

Copyright © 1998 LinguiSystems, Inc.

Division, *continued*

<table>
<tr><td>**Individual Objectives**</td><td>**Classroom Activities**</td></tr>
<tr><td>2. The student will know the division facts.</td><td>2. Teach the division facts at the same time as the multiplication facts so students see the reverse operations. Use manipulatives and/or color coding so students notice corresponding numbers.</td></tr>
</table>

$$\begin{array}{cc} & 3 \\ & \times 2 \\ \dfrac{3}{2\overline{)6}} & \overline{6} \end{array}$$

3. The student will understand the relationship between division and fractions.

3. Make several large circle patterns. Cut parts to fit on top of each circle, like halves, quarters, fifths, and eighths. First, discuss, for example, how many halves and quarters make a whole circle. Then, give sample word problems like the following:

A pizza was divided into eight pieces. Pick the circle that shows how the pizza was divided.

Five of the pieces were eaten. Write a fraction to show what part of the pizza was eaten.

4. The student will divide numbers with remainders.

4. Illustrate the concept of a remainder or a number "left over" with manipulatives first. For example, in dividing 11 by 5, make two even groups leaving a remainder of one. Write the division problem at the same time. Circle the remainder, then show students how to write the answer using *r* to indicate the remainder.

5. The student will divide with two-, three- and four-digit numbers.

5. Color highlight the corresponding number of digits in the divisor and dividend to show students how to get started. Then, have students work the problems on graph paper or paper with column indicators to help them learn how to arrange and shift numbers as they divide.

Copyright © 1998 LinguiSystems, Inc.

Division, *continued*

Individual Objectives	**Classroom Activities**

6. The student will learn the divisibility rules.

6. Create a game for students to practice recognizing divisibility. Write numbers on Bingo-like cards. As students correctly guess what number a number is divisible by, let them cover it with a card showing that number. At first, allow students to have the divisibility rules to refer to. Later, have students practice recognizing the rules independently.

7. The student will divide with decimals.

7. To make the problem less confusing visually, have students rewrite the problem after they've "shifted" decimals in the numbers. Using graph or columned paper will also help students keep track of where they are in a problem.

8. The student will divide fractions.

8. Teach division of fractions right after teaching students how to multiply them. Have students make strategy cards to refer to that list these rules:

   a. Rewrite the first fraction on the left exactly as it is.
   b. Rewrite the second fraction so the top and bottom numbers are opposite of the way they were.
   c. Then, follow the rules for multiplication of fractions.

9. The student will divide mixed numbers.

9. Review how to convert mixed numbers into "top heavy" or improper fractions. Then, have students follow the same strategy as for dividing fractions. First, give students problems that don't require cross multiplication, then one cross multiplication and then cross multiplication occurring for all numbers.

Copyright © 1998 LinguiSystems, Inc.

Fractions and Decimals

Individual Objectives

1. The student will understand the concepts of $\frac{1}{2}$, $\frac{1}{3}$, and $\frac{1}{4}$.

2. The student will recognize equivalent fractions.

3. The student will compare fractions.

4. The student will reduce a fraction to lowest terms.

5. The student will add fractions with like and unlike denominators.

Classroom Activities

1. Divide common shapes into halves, thirds and fourths. Have students color in a part of the shape, say "One out of two parts equals one-half" and write the fraction. Then, move on to using objects in groups of four, three and two. Have students show one out of four or one-fourth of a group, and so on. Write and say the fraction at the same time.

2. Make identically sized shapes to lay over each other to demonstrate equivalency. For example, a shape divided into fourths can be covered by two halves making the same sized shape to demonstrate that $\frac{2}{4} = \frac{1}{2}$.

3. Use divisible treats, like candy bars or a pan cookie. Divide one candy bar into three pieces, for example, and another into six pieces. Then, ask students if they'd prefer $\frac{1}{3}$ or $\frac{1}{6}$. They soon realize that the bigger the bottom number, the less food they get! Write fractions in order from smallest denominator to largest denominator to show the inverse relationship.

4. Have students show a multiplication fact for the numerator and denominator. Then, show them how to cross out the common divisor to get the reduced fraction.

$$\frac{3}{15} = \frac{\cancel{3} \times 1}{\cancel{3} \times 5} = \frac{1}{5}$$

5. Teach adding fractions using families of denominators, like 4, 8 and 12, so students can also see how fractions can be reduced. Later, give students problems with unlike denominators, but based on multiplication facts that are easy for them, like 5 x 4 or 3 x 6.

Fractions and Decimals, *continued*

Individual Objectives	**Classroom Activities**

6. The student will subtract fractions with like and unlike denominators.

6. Teach adding with like denominators first, especially in families of numbers, like halves and fourths, or fifths and tenths. Don't give students fraction answers that reduce until they master the addition concept. Then, progress to adding numbers with unlike denominators. Again, use problems based on recognizable number families.

7. The student will subtract fractions from whole numbers.

7. Remind students that the number one is represented by having the numerator and the denominator the same number. Show them several fractions so they can practice recognizing the number one in fraction form. Then, to work a subtraction problem, write on index cards the equivalent fractions for the whole number using the denominator of the fraction to be subtracted. For example, for the problem $5 - \frac{1}{4}$, you would have five index cards with $\frac{4}{4}$. Then, show students how the $\frac{1}{4}$ is taken from just one of the $\frac{4}{4}$ cards, leaving 4 cards and $\frac{3}{4}$.

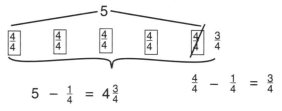

$$5 - \frac{1}{4} = 4\frac{3}{4} \qquad \frac{4}{4} - \frac{1}{4} = \frac{3}{4}$$

8. The student will add fractions and mixed numbers.

8. Students can usually handle adding the different fractions, but get confused converting the fractions into equivalent whole numbers and fractions. Before working such problems, have students convert improper fractions to mixed numbers as review.

9. The student will subtract fractions and mixed numbers.

9. With such complex processes, students may need a strategy card to refer to. Strategy steps might include:
   a. Change all fractions to have the same denominator.
   b. Add the fractions.
   c. Change any improper or "top-heavy" fractions into a whole number and a fraction.
   d. Add the whole numbers and bring down the fraction in your answer.

Copyright © 1998 LinguiSystems, Inc.

Fractions and Decimals, *continued*

Individual Objectives	**Classroom Activities**
10. The student will write a decimal as a fraction.	10. Teach students the rule about the relationship between zeros and decimal points. For example, to convert .345 to a fraction, students would say, "Three decimal points means three zeros, so .345 would equal $\frac{345}{1000}$."
11. The student will convert fractions to decimals.	11. Encourage students to memorize common decimal equivalents, like $\frac{3}{4}$ equals .75. Then, play a Concentration type game where several fractions and decimal equivalent pairs are placed facedown. Have students match the pairs. The student making the most matches wins.
12. The student will convert fractions and decimals to percents.	12. Teach percent equivalents only after students have memorized fraction and decimal equivalents. Then, show students how to move the decimal two places to the right to make a percent. For other fractions, show students how to divide the fraction and then convert to a percent by moving the decimal.
13. The student will increase an amount by a given percent.	13. Use real-life examples to illustrate when an amount would be increased by a percent. Discuss things like raises, inflation, or the increased value of a collectible, like a baseball card. Remind students to add the amount of the percentage increase to the original value of the item.
14. The student will decrease an amount by a given percent.	14. Have students highlight the words in a problem that indicate the value or cost of something has decreased. Remind students that any time a percentage of difference occurs, the problem involves a two-step process. After the number is found, the next step is either to add or subtract to find the answer.

Copyright © 1998 LinguiSystems, Inc.

Money

Individual Objectives

1. The student will recognize coins, bills and their values.

2. The student will write given amounts of money.

3. The student will count out money.

4. The student will put together different combinations of coins and/or bills to equal a given amount.

5. The student will solve basic word problems with money.

6. The student will match money words with written decimals.

Classroom Activities

1. Create a lotto matching game. Place cards with coin pictures on them facedown and have students turn over cards to match pairs of the same coin, stating their values.

2. Make imaginary trips to favorite stores. Let students list the items they would buy. Then, read amounts to students for the items while they write the numbers. For fun, have students "total" their bills.

3. Have students practice counting by fives, tens and twenty-fives. Then, give students actual amounts of money to count.

4. With play money, have students count aloud combinations of coins to equal the value of a given object, such as five nickels or two dimes and a nickel for a package of gum. Once students can count out coins, move on to combinations with bills.

5. Let students make up word problems around everyday situations at school. For example, students could estimate the total transportation, food and entertainment costs for a field trip. Have students exchange their problems for solving.

6. Make a large three-column chart on laminated paper labeled *Dollars, Dimes*, and *Cents*. Use real or pretend money to represent given amounts. Arrange the amounts under the correct columns, like four dollar bills, six dimes and three pennies. As different amounts are placed in columns, have students read the numbers. Numbers can be written in washable marker above the amounts. When students understand equivalent amounts, go on to using quarters and nickels in the cents columns, explaining how it's written to take up two columns. For example, three quarters equals seven dimes and five cents.

Money, *continued*

Individual Objectives

7. The student will read words representing dollars and cents through the hundreds.

8. The student will write dollars and cents through hundreds upon hearing them.

9. The student will make change from $1, $5, $10, and $20.

Classroom Activities

7. Create a large chart labeled *Hundreds, Tens, Ones,* and *Cents*. Make word cards to fit in each column. Students can then make their own numbers and challenge other students to read the amount correctly. For example, a student could represent $425 with the word cards four hundred, twenty, five, and dollars.

8. Make fake checks for students to fill in. Then, have students write in the correct amounts as you describe buying situations. For example, students could write a check for five dollars and sixty cents for the extra-long shower they took that morning!

9. Simulate purchasing situations for students, such as paying a bill at a restaurant. First, have students estimate what they think the change should be. Then, with play or real money, have them count back to the original amount to make correct change.

Time and Measurement ··

1. The student will recognize the hours.

2. The student will learn the purposes of different kinds of clocks, like digital clocks, stopwatches and alarm clocks.

3. The student will tell time to the hour.

1. Draw a large clock face on the chalkboard. Then, have students stand and move their arms to represent the hours. The left arm is the longer hand and stays at 12 o'clock, while the right hand moves to the hours. Switch arms at 6 o'clock. Have students say what time it is as their hands move.

2. Design classroom activities to demonstrate the use of each kind of clock. The alarm clock could be set to signal when to shift to a new activity or the stopwatch could be used to time how long it takes to put materials away.

3. Help students learn to tell time using both a clock and a wristwatch. Let students take turns wearing a wristwatch. Have them keep track of the time, for example, for reading class or for recess.

Copyright © 1998 LinguiSystems, Inc.

Individual Objectives

Classroom Activities

4. The student will tell time to the five minutes.

4. Make several large clock faces with five-minute segments. Use different highlight colors to color in five minutes on one clock, ten minutes, twenty-five minutes, and so on. Stress the dividing marks between each segment. Then, play memory games with the clocks. Flash the fifteen-minute clock and have students color in a clock appropriately on a worksheet with enlarged clock faces.

5. The student will write time in various ways, like 5 P.M., 5 o'clock, 5:00.

5. Place a digital and hand clock near each other so students can see how the time representations are different. Initially, focus only on counting minutes after the hour and using consistent language to describe it, such as fifteen minutes after four.

6. The student will recognize A.M. hours and P.M. hours.

6. Change the appearance of the clock in your room for P.M. hours. For example, you could put a dark blue background or border around the clock. Discuss what happens in P.M. hours, such as leaving school, eating supper, and going to bed.

7. The student will understand and apply the terms *clockwise* and *counterclockwise*.

7. Draw a large clock face outside on the playground. Have a student stand inside it with arms outstretched like the hands of a clock. Students can take turns moving clockwise and counterclockwise. Discuss typical uses of the terms, such as for opening a locker or a jar, or for turning a key in a lock.

8. The student will list the days of the week.

8. Play a memorizing game. Challenge students to develop a memory cue, such as drawing the sun for Sunday, the number *2* for Tuesday, and so on to help them memorize the days.

Copyright © 1998 LinguiSystems, Inc.

Time and Measurement, *continued*

Individual Objectives

9. The student will understand the relationship between minutes, hours, a day, a week, a month, and a year.

Classroom Activities

9. Discuss and conduct activities that reflect the time amount you're teaching. Then, record the events on a chart to hang in your room.

Min.	Hrs.	Yr.
Eat breakfast 5 min.	Gym class 1 hr.	Grow long hair 1 yr.
Bus ride 20 min.	Lunch and recess 1 hr.	Save for bike 1 yr.
Read picture book 15 min.	Visit to zoo 2 hrs.	Finish grade 2 1 yr.

10. The student will convert units of time, like minutes to hours.

10. Use paper cups or cans labeled with the conversion amount. For example, a day is twenty-four hours. Give students slips of paper or small objects to represent hours. Then, have them convert 48 hours, for example, to the amount of days (2) by counting into the can 24 hour slips two times.

11. The student will know facts related to the calendar, like days, weeks, months, and seasons in a year.

11. Even at a young age, students can begin to use a planning calendar for their own purposes. At the beginning of each month, have students indicate upcoming events on their individual calendars. For example, a visit to the dentist's office might be scheduled Friday, while cousin Alejandro might be visiting in two weeks. Have students share their calendars with their families to add and verify scheduled events. Then, discuss the events in class, as well as the effect seasons and weather may have on their activities.

12. The student will understand use of a time card.

12. Create time cards for your students. When they begin and end work, like an assignment, have them write the time on the card. If possible, have them figure out the time they worked.

Copyright © 1998 LinguiSystems, Inc.

Time and Measurement, *continued*

Individual Objectives	**Classroom Activities**
13. The student will learn basic measurements of length and weight.	13. Invite your school nurse to weigh and measure your students and record the data on a personal information sheet. Later in the year, repeat this activity and compare growth made. To visually illustrate students' height and weight, bring in enough canned food to equal 60 pounds, for example, or stack cereal boxes high enough to equal a student's height. Then, donate the "food measurers" to a food pantry!
14. The student will write abbreviations for measurements, like *ft.* and *lb.*	14. Make up silly sentences for students to practice listening and writing abbreviations, such as "Gordon's gator was 10 feet and 2 inches long." As you read, ask students to write what they hear.
15. The student will know the value of a dozen and half dozen.	15. Put together different combinations of things to illustrate *dozen* and *half dozen*. For example, three students would have half a dozen feet or there are a dozen balls to play with at recess time. (Bring the balls into your classroom to show them!)
16. The student will measure units of length using a ruler, yardstick or tape measure.	16. Give students various objects to measure with a ruler, yardstick and tape measure. Have them measure each thing with each device. For example, students could measure the length of the room, the depths of the inside of their desks or the distance around the big drum in the music room. Follow up with a discussion about how you decide which measuring device to use.
17. The student will convert units of length, like inches to feet, feet to yards.	17. Make paper measuring devices that can be laid on top of each other to visualize relationships and conversions. For example, after measuring the height of the pencil sharpener on the wall with a yard length, have students convert it to feet by laying feet lengths on top of the yard lengths.

Copyright © 1998 LinguiSystems, Inc.

Individual Objectives   **Classroom Activities**

18. The student will measure with units of liquid measurement, like cup, pint and quart.

18. Use items like rice, beans or dried corn to fill liquid measuring items. Have students compare the amount in a cup with the amount in a quart. Give them a chart to refer to showing the equivalent cups in a pint, and so on, and allow them to pour items back and forth. Eventually, let students apply their skills by making no-bake items like Kool-Aid® or pudding.

19. The student will measure units of weight.

19. Bring in a food scale and a bathroom scale and let students measure items in the room. On butcher paper, record the name of the object and its weight. After some practice, have pairs of students estimate the weight of objects, verify their estimates by actual weighing and then record their findings on the butcher paper. Discuss circumstances under which it's important to know weight, such as for personal growth records, planning recipes or mailing items.

20. The student will convert units of weight, like ounces to pounds, pounds to tons.

20. Let students visit a store called The Megaton Candy Store where they can buy to their hearts' delight. Create candy selections that range from ounces for very special candy to tons for others. Allot students a choice of one ton and six hundred pounds of candy each. Students then have to decide which candies to buy and add up their purchases. For extra fun, put a price per pound or ton and have students calculate their expenses.

Word Problems ....

1. The student will isolate important information to solve a word problem.

1. Place word problems on an overhead projector. Have students conclude what they're asked to find and circle the important information for answering it. Numbers needed for computation later can be written off to the side of the problem where they appear, in addition to a sign indicating the process to be used.

Individual Objectives	**Classroom Activities**

2. The student will recognize words like *total*, *sum* and *in all* as signals to add.

2. With a highlight pen, students code words in a set of word problems that indicate adding and then solve the problems.

3. The student will recognize words like *how many fewer*, *less than* and *take away* as signals to subtract.

3. With a marker, students search for subtraction words and then write the minus sign above them. They should also circle the numbers to be used to solve the problem.

4. The student will write equations for word problems.

4. Present word problems orally to your students and ask them to write an equation with pictures and symbols to solve the problem. Then, try a combination of words and symbols to suggest an equation, eventually using just symbols.

Example: Ms. Garcia had five pencils in her pencil holder. Three students borrowed pencils in class. How many pencils were left in her pencil holder?

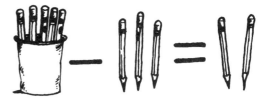

5. The student will do word problems with fractions.

5. Students need to recognize words that indicate part of something is being used, such as items were divided into two equal groups (1/2), or 9 of 12 students returned their parent permission forms. Have students highlight or circle the numbers and the words indicating fractions.

Real-life Situations ··

1. The student will put together the correct coins to pay for a priced object.

1. Select five objects, like a pencil and a coloring book. Put prices on them and have students match needed coins to the price.

2. The student will use a calendar for planning.

2. Given a blank monthly calendar, students record important events, like birthdays, special school events, visits to Mom or Dad, and days of favorite TV shows or activities.

31

Copyright © 1998 LinguiSystems, Inc.

Real-life Situations, *continued*

Individual Objectives	Classroom Activities
3. The student will apply understanding of % to everyday situations.	3. Have students solve word problems describing two similar items on sale. Use % off to choose the better buy.
4. The student will write checks and record them accurately in a checkbook register	4. "Visit" a mall and make simulated purchases. Write a check for each given purchase and record it in the checkbook register.
5. The student will fill in a simple tax form.	5. Get actual federal tax forms for students as well as examples of W-2 forms and paycheck stubs so students understand where the information comes from. Then, give each student the information for a different worker. Choose an "expert" on taxes from your classroom to be an accountant or the IRS that reviews the form for accuracy.
6. The student will read prices.	6. Students need to be aware that prices may appear in several places. Products may be bar coded or items will be priced by a shelf sign near them. Some products, like grocery items, may have the item price as well as a per unit price. For example, cereals might have a price per ounce. Visiting a combination grocery and department store would be a valuable experience for learning about pricing.
7. The student will understand the concepts of *most expensive* and *cheapest*.	7. Have students read ads for similar products and make a chart listing the features of the items, like CD/tape players. Then, based on a judgment of the quality of each product and its features, they can decide which is the best buy.
8. The student will add and subtract time related to everyday situations.	8. Whenever students change to a new activity, give them a time limit for its accomplishment. Have students figure what time that will be. Clock boards with movable hands can be used to check their answers.

Copyright © 1998 LinguiSystems, Inc.

Geometrical Shapes and Concepts ....

Individual Objectives

1. The student will recognize similar shapes.

2. The student will recognize flat shapes, like a triangle and circle.

3. The student will recognize solid shapes, like cubes and spheres.

4. The student will recognize fraction of a shape, like $\frac{1}{2}$ a circle.

5. The student will find the perimeter of common shapes, like squares and rectangles.

Classroom Activities

1. After a lesson discussing different attributes of shapes, have pairs of students take turns grouping some small everyday objects and sharing their reasoning. Then, move on to activity sheets using pictorial representations of shapes where students match similar objects.

2. Make outline shapes of geometric shapes. Then, send pairs of students to different school locations to find and list items that match their shapes. For example, students sent to the music room might find drums and cymbals for circles, or a piano or xylophone for a rectangle. Follow up with a class discussion where teams justify their matches.

3. Make patterns for students to construct three-dimensional shapes, like cubes, spheres, cylinders, and prisms. Then, play review games where you toss the shape to a student and ask a question, like "What's the name of this object? How many sides does it have?" or "What is something in the (cafeteria) shaped like this?" Encourage students to make up their own questions and games.

4. Constructing shapes and fractions of shapes from construction paper allows students to see the relationship of one part to another. Use different colors for different parts. For example, students can visualize $\frac{1}{2}$ better if they see $\frac{1}{2}$ of a circle in yellow placed over a red, whole circle.

5. Cut different strips of colored paper in even inch measurements for students to make shapes from, like three strips for a triangle. Then, have students measure the strips and add the numbers to get the perimeter.

Copyright © 1998 LinguiSystems, Inc.

Geometrical Shapes and Concepts, *continued*

Individual Objectives

6. The student will find the area of common shapes, like squares and rectangles.

7. The student will use a number line.

8. The student will understand the difference between positive and negative numbers.

9. The student will add, subtract, multiply, or divide positive and negative numbers.

Classroom Activities

6. Contrast the concept of area to perimeter by teaching both at the same time. Make large shapes to lay out on a floor or table, like a rectangle that is three feet by four feet. Draw in the three by four squares that make up the inside area and show students how the area is found by multiplying the sides. Demonstrate how the number found by multiplying equals the total of the inner squares. Have students then find the perimeter by adding the outer dimensions, 3 + 4 + 3 + 4.

7. Make large-sized number lines that students can keep in folders for use or attach to their desks. Provide tokens the students can place on the number line when learning a concept. For example, they can place a token on 4 and then move 2 spaces toward 0 to illustrate "four take away two" or 4 – 2 = 2. Reinforce the relationships of the numbers in the calculation by saying, "The number is getting bigger as you go to the right or add" or "The number is decreasing or getting smaller as you go to the left or subtract."

8. Create a board game using the number line as its path. Cards can say things like, "Move ahead three spaces" or "Uh-oh, back to zero!" Before students move, they have to say if they're moving in a positive or negative direction. Then, create simple word problems, such as "The price of a hamburger decreased 5 cents today" or "The gym teacher made us do 8 more sit-ups in class" so they can apply the skill to real-life.

9. Use number lines for students to move numbers in positive and negative directions as they learn to add and subtract them. For all the operations, students will need visual reminders about the rules for signs once they've computed an answer. Have students make an individual index card for each math operation that illustrates the signs like the example on the next page.

Individual Objectives

Classroom Activities

Multiplying

$$+\ 5$$
$$\underline{x\ +\ 5}$$
$$+25$$

$$-\ 6$$
$$\underline{x\ -\ 7}$$
$$+42$$

If the signs are alike, the answer is +.

---

10. The student will read and make a pictograph, circle, bar, and line graph.

10. When students learn about each kind of graph, use the same data to make each graph. For example, students might conduct a survey about their favorite and least favorite things about school. Then, each kind of graph could be made to report their findings. Students could compare the ease of reading one kind of graph over another.

11. The student will use a calculator.

11. Use of the calculator will be critical when students are learning to add decimals and money, as well as when they learn the concept of rounding off. Once the student has learned a particular skill, allow him to use it to check and critically evaluate his answers.

12. The student will carry out computations using a variety of devices, like a cash register, the adding function on a computer or an adding machine.

12. Let students practice new skills in a variety of ways. For example, using an adding machine or a cash register are excellent ways to reinforce decimal or money-adding skills.

13. The student will use software to reinforce math skills.

13. Expose students to commercially-available software that helps them learn as well as practice a skill. Software programs are also available that can be tailored to the student's current level of math functioning.

14. The student will apply a variety of math skills in real-life situations.

14. The best application of skills occurs when students have to think through how to handle real-life situations. Many problem-solving based, interactive board games exist to practice and apply new skills, like budgeting or handling credit cards.

Copyright © 1998 LinguiSystems, Inc.

Reading

Today, Adam needs help with his history assignment. Together we look at the types of questions he's expected to answer. As I read a question, Adam repeats the key words or main idea. Then, he scans the chapter for headings related to these key words. Once found, he reads a section aloud, getting some words, and stumbling over others that I eventually pronounce for him. Finally, Adam paraphrases the ideas and writes his answer to the question.

It is a lengthy process to answer just one question and many students have neither the skills, nor the motivation or persistence to stick with it. Consequently, assignments are incomplete. And despite having quizzes or tests read to them as an accommodation in the regular education classroom, many of these students fail. They do not fail because they lack the intelligence to handle the class curriculum. They fail because they lack the variety of reading strategies they need to tackle a history book, a storybook, or a driver's education manual.

The objectives and activities that follow will help your students develop strategies in the areas of:

- Phonic and Word Recognition Skills
    - Auditory Discrimination
    - Auditory Memory
    - Visual Memory and Discrimination
- Reading for Pleasure
- Reading Comprehension
- Content Area Reading
- Vocabulary

Copyright © 1998 LinguiSystems, Inc.

Reading

Yearly Goal: to improve phonic and word recognition skills

Phonic and Word Recognition Skills

Auditory Discrimination

Individual Objectives

1. The student will identify common sounds.

2. The student will remember a pattern of sounds.

3. The student will recognize words with the same beginning sound.

4. The student will recognize the final sounds of *n, d, k, m, t,* and *p.*

Classroom Activities

1. Together with students, make a tape of common sounds, like musical sounds, animal sounds and environmental sounds. Then, let students listen to the tape and identify the sounds. Initially, group similar sounds together to make identification easier, but then mix them at random later to test students' discrimination and memory skills.

2. Make sound-producing instruments from a variety of odds and ends, like buttons in a jar or macaroni in a small matchbox. Use easy-to-handle musical instruments, like a tambourine or maracas, too. Let the student handle the items and listen to the sounds first. Next, have the student turn her chair and face away from you while you create a pattern of sounds. Then, have the student turn around and duplicate the pattern she heard.

3. Read a series of words to your students which all begin with the same consonant except for one. Have students either tell you what sound they hear or choose the correct letter from two letter cards. Some students may need the letter and sound choices presented before listening to the words.

4. With word and picture cards, have students distinguish between two endings. Begin with more distinct sounds, like *n* and *p,* later progressing to sounds that are harder to discriminate, like *m* and *n.*

Copyright © 1998 LinguiSystems, Inc.

Individual Objectives

Classroom Activities

5. The student will discriminate ending consonant sounds.

5. Make up a very short story or sets of sentences that include words with one or two target ending sounds. As students listen, have them circle words ending with the same sound.

6. The student will recognize words with double consonant patterns, like *rolling* and *stopping*.

6. Many words with double consonant patterns are two-syllable words. Make two-piece puzzles where students have to match the first part of the word with the second and then read it aloud. For extra practice, have students make up verses with end rhyme using double consonant words.

7. The student will learn common words with silent consonants, like *l, t, k, h, b, gh, w*, and *ph (f)*.

7. Make a huge wall poster that students can add words to. Under each silent letter or letter combination, have students write words with silent consonants as they discover them. Students might write words like, *phone* and *elephant* for *ph*, or *dough* and *bough* for *gh*.

8. The student will recognize the initial sound blends of *st, pl, bl, br, tr, dr, gr*, and *fr*.

8. Make an audiotape of short sentences using words familiar to your students. Include words that begin with sound blends. Prepare a printed copy of the sentences, too. As students listen, they circle targeted initial sound blends.

   a. Steve played with the truck.
   b. Grilled cheese sounds great for lunch.
   c. The students drove their fourth grade teacher crazy!

9. The student will recognize the initial sound blends of *cr, sn, sl, pr*, and *cl*.

9. Provide pictures of objects, people or places whose names begin with a blend, like *clown, clip, snail, sneaker*, and *crown*. Then, have students sort the pictures into blend piles.

10. The student will recognize the initial consonant blends of *thr, gl, squ, apr*, and *str*.

10. Make up silly sentences or stories using blends and print them in large letters on an overhead projector. Read the sentences or stories aloud. Then, have students take turns circling the blends in the sentences on the overhead. (See the examples on the next page.)

Individual Objectives

Classroom Activities

Examples:
   In April, it rained a lot of squids and other
     strange creatures.
   Three strong people put the squids in a
     square glass tank.
   The squids are a very strange sight to see!

11. The student will know the hard and soft sounds produced by *c* (*s* and *k* sounds) and *g* (*g* and *j* sounds).

11. For each letter, have students make hard and soft sound cards. Glue cotton balls on the soft sound cards and sand or dried macaroni on the hard sound cards. Let students add a picture to illustrate a word that starts with the sound if they'd like. Then, read aloud separate words. As students hear each word, have them hold up the correct hard or soft sound card. Later, have students notice if there's any consistent spelling patterns in words that have hard or soft sounds.

12. The student will learn the various sounds of *y*.

12. Make picture cards with *y* words, like *good-bye* and *baby*, to show the long and short sounds of *y*. Emphasize learning what a word looks like in order to recognize it rather than relying on sounding it out when a letter has two possible sounds. Color code the *y* that sounds like *i* one color, and the *y* that sounds like *e* another color as you write the words.

13. The student will recognize short vowel sounds in words.

13. Make sound pictures for a letter, like a baseball cap for short *a*. Listen to a story or a musical tape with some short *a* words. Hold up your picture for short *a*.

14. The student will identify CVC words as short vowel words.

14. Give students separate cards containing vowels and consonants. Have them put together two consonants and a vowel to form a recognizable short vowel word.

Copyright © 1998 LinguiSystems, Inc.

Individual Objectives

Classroom Activities

15. The student will discriminate between long and short vowel sounds.

15. As you read aloud words with long vowel sounds, over exaggerate and lengthen the sound. Do the opposite for short vowel sound words. Have students make index cards, one with a long vowel on it and the other with a short vowel. As you read words, students choose the correct card to match the vowel sound.

16. The student will learn the different sounds of vowel digraphs, like *ee, ea, ai*, and *oa*.

16. Teach the vowel digraphs immediately after teaching long vowel sounds. Reinforce the rule, "When two vowels go walking, the first one does the talking." Let students exaggerate the long sounds in each word, like the *o* in *boat*, or the *e* in *deer*.

17. The student will recognize the *er, ir*, and *ar* sounds in words.

17. On large poster board, make clusters of words using each sound, like *water, sister, bird, stir, car*, and *mark*. Circle the sounds in each word. Have students notice how similar the *ir* and *er* sounds are, while the *ar* sound is unique.

18. The student will learn the sounds of diphthongs, like *ou, ow, or, oy, aw*, and *au*.

18. Teach similar sound pairs at the same time, like *aw/au* and *ou/ow*. Stress the need to learn the spelling that matches the diphthong in a particular word.

19. The student will read digraphs, like *ph, gh, tch*, and *qu* in more difficult words.

19. Play a game of Sounds in Disguise! First, teach students the "disguised sounds," like the *f* sound for *ph* in *phone* and *gh* in *laugh*. Then, have students draw a word from a bag and read it using its disguised sound. Award points or give rewards for recognizing words with unusual digraphs.

20. The student will recognize word endings that change meaning, like *s, ed* and *ing*.

20. Teach verbs and verb tenses. First, have students dictate sentences describing action. Place each sentence in the correct spot under a three-column chart labeled *Past, Present* and *Future*. Then, have students notice the pattern to endings appearing in each column, like *-ed* signals *Past*.

Copyright © 1998 LinguiSystems, Inc.

Individual Objectives	**Classroom Activities**
21. The student will recognize words that rhyme.	21. Using highly predictable rhyming books, read rhymes aloud, but allow students to supply the missing rhyming word in the pair.
22. The student will identify the number of syllables in a word.	22. Emphasize the importance of hearing syllables while learning to spell a word. Provide cards with words divided in two or more ways. Have students choose the correct set to match the pronunciation of the word. Then, ask students to spell the word orally or in writing.
23. The student will recognize when a prefix or suffix has been added.	23. Teach students common prefixes, like *in, im*, and *re*, and suffixes, like *ment, tion*, and *able*. Then, play an auditory recognition game. As you read familiar words, have students answer "Prefix added, Suffix added," or "No change." Students then need to identify and spell what was added.

Auditory Memory

1. The student will repeat a series of words in sequence.	1. Begin with words that are related so an element of meaning is attached, like days of the week or flavors of ice cream. Then, increase the memory task by using fewer related words and later gradually increasing the number of words to be repeated.
2. The student will follow a series of oral directions correctly.	2. Create individual pictures to depict each step in a set of oral directions. Say the directions and then have students correctly sequence the pictures. Discuss what happens if directions are followed out of order.
3. The student will recall details from a past class experience or discussion.	3. As a lead-in to the day's lesson, have a student summarize events from the previous day. Challenge the student to remember everything she can before other class members are allowed to add details.

Copyright © 1998 LinguiSystems, Inc.

Auditory Memory, *continued*

Individual Objectives

4. The student will remember and relay oral messages, like a phone message.

Classroom Activities

4. Simulate telephone calls with play phones (even with the big kids!). Students then "take" messages by either remembering them or jotting down pertinent details following the phone call. Don't allow them to ask the caller to dictate word by word messages.

Visual Memory and Discrimination ....

1. The student will match objects and pictures by color, shape or design.

1. Make or purchase color, shape and design cards. Include cards with similar shapes or designs, but different colors, for example, so students can do different levels of visual discrimination. Then, arrange the cards in patterns and have students copy the patterns.

2. The student will match letters, numbers or words.

2. Play a game of Match Up. Make duplicate cards for individual letters, numbers and frequently used sight words. Place one set of letter cards, like *b, s, f, r,* and *t,* in a bag. Give the other set to the student. Have the student draw cards one at a time and match it with the same letter. Make the game more difficult by increasing the number of letters in the bag or including visually similar cards, like *b* and *d*, or *m* and *n*. Play different games for numbers and then for words.

3. The student will copy patterns from a visual model.

3. Using colored pegs and a peg board, arrange pegs in various patterns. Have students copy a row by arranging one immediately below the given row. Progress from simple to more complex arrangements.

4. The student will copy letters from a visual model.

4. Using a flannel board or magnetic letters, have students arrange letters to duplicate a visual model. As students are ready, have them write the letters below a model on the chalkboard or overhead, progressing to being able to copy in writing on their own paper.

Copyright © 1998 LinguiSystems, Inc.

Visual Memory and Discrimination, *continued*

Individual Objectives

5. The student will copy words from a visual model.

6. The student will copy patterns independently.

7. The student will copy letters independently.

8. The student will copy words independently.

9. The student will point out certain objects within a design.

10. The student will recall details from a picture.

11. The student will tell the difference between capital and lower case letters.

Classroom Activities

5. Follow the directions for the activity above, having students copy words with meaning for them, like their names, teachers' names, the school name, and so on.

6. Using shapes students are able to copy, like circles, triangles and squares, make patterns. Have students draw the shapes and then color them as they'd like.

7. Provide letter models that are color-cued to help students recognize distinct features of letters. For example, one color could represent the straight line in the letter *d*, while another color is used to write the rounded part.

8. As a class, write very short sentences about something you did that day. Then, provide letter cards for students to arrange into words to duplicate their sentences. Later, have students progress to copying words in their own writing.

9. To develop more complex visual discrimination skills, give students practice with activities, like hidden picture puzzles and Find Waldo type activities.

10. Work on listening and visual memory skills simultaneously by having students work in pairs to remember the details of a picture. Place a photo or picture facedown in front of one student. The student has one minute to remember everything he sees. Then, the student tells the other student what he remembers. If the student gets stuck, the other student may give him clues. Move from basic pictures to pictures with more activity and details.

11. Teach students when capital letters are used, like for people's names, names of special places and city names. Then, review the letter pairs, like *Aa*, emphasizing how the *A* is large because it has a more important job than the lower case *a*.

Visual Memory and Discrimination, *continued*

Individual Objectives	Classroom Activities
12. The student will recognize the configuration of words.	12. Using short sentences with familiar words, outline in color the configurations of individual words. Then, provide cards with the same words and some close in shape. Students must choose the correct words and arrange them in a sentence.
13. The student will alphabetize words by the first letter.	13. Make large, individual alphabet cards and have students arrange them vertically on a large desk or the floor. Initially, give students only a few letters to use at a time. Then, give students familiar words to alphabetize. Have them color highlight the first letter in each word and place each word near the correct letter of the alphabet.
14. The student will alphabetize words using the second letter.	14. To practice alphabetizing to the second letter, modify the activity for alphabetizing words to the first letter. Have students color highlight the first two letters of a word and then place them in order by the correct letter card. To simplify the task, you may need to make cards that include the letter and a vowel and arrange them in order, like *ha-, he-, hi-, ho-,* and *hu-.* Students can then place words in order within a letter "category."
15. The student will recognize word endings that show: • more than one (*s, es*) • past time (*ed*) • ownership (*'s, s'*) • contractions	15. Make word cards and word ending cards that students can manipulate to make variations of a word. For example, students can change *shoe* to *shoes, jump* to *jumped* and *is not* to *isn't.* Have students make up sentences to go with the words.
16. The student will recognize compound words.	16. Using words familiar to your students, make large individual word cards that can be combined to form compound words, like *back/pack, book/bag, note/book,* and *base/ball.* Give teams identical sets of cards and challenge them to come up with a variety of combinations.

Visual Memory and Discrimination, *continued*

Individual Objectives

17. The student will read hyphenated words.

18. The student will use context clues to analyze new words.

19. The student will recognize root words.

20. The student will recognize commonly used sight words.

21. The student will tell the difference between homophone pairs, like *new/knew, hear/here,* and *there/their/they're.*

22. The student will develop good reading habits through oral reading and self-correcting.

Classroom Activities

17. When students see a hyphenated word, have them write down the first part of the word. Then, have them add the second part of the word from the next line before they attempt to pronounce the word.

18. Have students first notice features of the word, like prefixes, suffixes or its beginning letters. Then, have them read the sentence containing the word to pick up context clues that might aid in discovering its meaning and pronunciation.

19. Play a game of Root Loot. Challenge students to find as many variations of root words, like *play* and *book*, as they can using prefixes, suffixes and compound words. As students think of words, have them write the words on cards and put their "loot" in a bag. To make the game more challenging, have students think of their own root words.

20. Analyze students' writing for common sight words they use in their writing, but don't yet spell correctly. Make flash cards of these words and review five daily until students have mastered an entire list, like the Dolch Basic Sight Vocabulary.

21. Using word cards, teach students the different meanings of each homophone in a pair along with its spelling. Then, read sentences aloud to your students and have them identify which homophone fits the sentence. Present sentences visually, also, as needed.

22. Using a tape recorder, have the student read aloud a favorite book. Later, have the student listen to the tape, pausing the tape to verbally self-correct an error and then continue listening. Allow the student to read the book aloud again into a tape recorder to increase fluency and accuracy.

Copyright © 1998 LinguiSystems, Inc.

Visual Memory and Discrimination, *continued*

Individual Objectives	Classroom Activities
23. The student will learn to self-correct when reading aloud.	23. Create a tally sheet for self-monitoring. Then, play a game of "I Caught It" whose objective is for students to self-correct on words initially not recognized. As the student reads aloud, the teacher records words correct, words self-corrected and words mispronounced. Encourage students to read over the passage before playing the game.
24. The student will read aloud fluently.	24. Recruit volunteers, like parents, the principal or cooks to listen to your students read. After a student has read through a book at least once, he can request a listener.
25. The student will read aloud using tone/inflection appropriate to the reading material.	25. Choose a short play to read. Have students skim their parts for feelings and actions described in parentheses for the character as well as the type of punctuation at the end of the character's script. Then, students should attempt to read the play with feeling and realism.
26. The student will develop independent strategies for silent reading.	26. Students with learning disabilities often rely on having material read aloud to them, so consequently don't develop their own strategies. Provide silent reading time in class. Have students keep journals of what they discover about their own reading styles, such as "I need to read aloud to myself" or "Holding a card under the line helps me keep my place."

Yearly Goal: to read for pleasure and develop an interest in reading

Reading for Pleasure

1. The student will retell personal experiences in chronological order.	1. On a regular basis, have students share personal experiences. As a student talks, summarize the events she describes on an 8" x 11" piece of white paper. Include only one event per page. Then, read the events back to the student and have her place the events in order. Pages can be taped in sequence on a chalkboard.

Copyright © 1998 LinguiSystems, Inc.

Reading for Pleasure, *continued*

Individual Objectives	**Classroom Activities**
2. The student will read during class free time.	2. Establish a regular free reading time of 10 to 15 minutes. Allow students to choose their reading material and where they read. Reward with points for choosing their own books, getting started right away, and reading the entire time. Follow up with a short sharing time of what students learned or what interested them in their reading.
3. The student will read outside of class.	3. Make a reading booklet where students record reading done outside of class. Students can also write a one-sentence reaction to their reading. A parent or study hall teacher can sign off on the reading. Let students design and personalize their reading logs.
4. The student will choose and sustain the reading of an appropriate book.	4. Have students make a list of things they like to read or learn about. Then, have them take their lists to the library to help make a book choice. Give students plenty of time to look at books and read through a couple of pages before narrowing their choices.
5. The student will expand reading interests.	5. Readers build reading skills by applying them to a variety of reading material. Offer incentives or free time to encourage your students to explore new materials. If a student likes to read mysteries, for example, encourage the student to read not only about fictional mysteries, but also about unexplained mysteries in real life. Follow with discussions to compare and contrast what was learned.
6. The student will select his own reading material.	6. Create individual library boxes for each student in your classroom. Have students bring books, magazines and news articles from home appropriate to their needs, interests and abilities. Add surprise reading material to their boxes to expand their interests as well as develop current interests.

Copyright © 1998 LinguiSystems, Inc.

Reading Comprehension ....

Individual Objectives

1. The student will recognize the difference between fantasy and reality.

2. The student will distinguish between fact and fiction.

3. The student will identify the author's purpose.

4. The student will recognize the difference between fiction and nonfiction.

Classroom Activities

1. Make up situations and things for students to distinguish as real or fantasy. Students can make a "thumbs up" sign for real and "thumbs down" sign for fantasy. Encourage discussion over what students judge fantasy, but may become reality one day. For example, spaceships and space flight were once thought to be fantasy creations of the mind.

2. Create fact and fiction lists about your school like the one below.

Fact	Fiction
400 students	no homework
three-stories high	built on a gold mine
Ms. Schrader is the principal.	Michael Jordan went to school there.

   Discuss how factual information is provable by sight or measurement, while fiction is true only in one's mind.

3. Make cards labeled *To Entertain, To Inform* and *To Persuade*. On strips of paper, provide examples of specific current media material, like a radio commercial against drug use or an ad for an upcoming rock concert. Then, have students identify author's purpose by placing the strip under the correct card. Strips can even be placed between cards, if students justify their reasoning.

4. Read a variety of materials with your students, like short novels, news features and magazine articles. Have students read the title of each work and then scan the table of contents or chapter titles if they're available. Ask students to categorize the material as fiction or nonfiction and to note the type of language used.

Copyright © 1998 LinguiSystems, Inc.

Reading Comprehension, *continued*

Individual Objectives	**Classroom Activities**

5. The student will recognize figurative use of language.

5. Most figurative language is used to compare new experiences or objects to more familiar ones. Create a list of sensory statements for students to fill in and encourage them to think of a variety of descriptors for each one.

   Examples:
   The snow looked like ____.
   When the rocket took off, it sounded as if ____.
   Josh was so scared he looked like ____.
   Starting at a new school is as ____.

   Then, teach students the appropriate terminology for their comparisons, like *metaphor* or *simile*.

6. The student will recognize formal language.

6. Have students read a selection from their history book about an historical event and then excerpts from a short novel. For example, students could read about pioneer times and then compare it to a passage from a Laura Ingalls Wilder book. Have students note the types of words used and the tone of each selection.

7. The student will identify the mood of a reading selection.

7. Apply the concept of mood to fiction as well as nonfiction, such as a human interest story designed to arouse the reader's sympathy or compassion.

8. The student will predict outcomes.

8. Have students share personal experiences frequently. Before ending a story, though, stop the student who's sharing and have other students predict the outcome. List their ideas on the board and discuss the probability of their predictions. Then, let the student end her story.

9. The student will identify the cause of a situation.

9. Have students brainstorm and list every detail they know about an important situation in a story. Then, let students work in pairs to list causes for the situation. Follow with a discussion of the reasonableness of their causes.

Copyright © 1998 LinguiSystems, Inc.

Individual Objectives	**Classroom Activities**

Individual Objectives

10. The student will identify the effect of a certain action.

11. The student will state the main problem in a story.

12. The student will predict the ending of a story.

13. The student will identify details most important to the plot.

Classroom Activities

10. Stop midway in a story at the point when a main character is making a critical decision. Create three possible scenarios that sets of students can role-play to illustrate possible effects of the character's action. Then, have the class vote on the most logical choice and explain their thinking.

11. Provide students with cards indicating possible choices to fill in, such as:

    • The problem is between the character ____ and the character ____. I think this because ____.
    • The problem is between the character ____ and the thing ____. I think this because ____.
    • The problem is between the character ____ and the decision about ____ that he has to make for himself. I think this because ____.
    • The problem is between the character ____ and a ____ in nature. I think this because ____.

    Provide students with the descriptive names of problems or conflicts, like man vs. man, and man vs. nature, if they're ready. Have students make predictions about how the problem will get solved.

12. Provide students with ending options. In groups, let them discuss the likelihood of each ending and the story details that led them to their conclusions.

13. Have students make a Detail Guide to use as they read. Ask students to jot down any details they remember from the story and then check the Very Important box or leave the box blank to rate the significance of the detail to the plot. For example:

Detail	**Very Important**
Max accidentally left his keys in the lock.	❑

Reading Comprehension, *continued*

| **Individual Objectives** | **Classroom Activities** |

14. The student will understand and answer comprehension questions.

14. Provide written study guides for students to follow as they read. The guides should have students fill in important details about a story by asking *who, what, where, when, why*, and *how* questions. Before students answer, they should underline the information asked for so they can answer correctly.

15. The student will understand the use of quotation marks in reading.

15. Pair students and let them make up a short conversation. Students could tape record what they say and then write it later. Review the rules about indenting for a new speaker and using quotation marks or "talking marks" around what was said.

16. The student will identify the purpose of paragraphing in dialogue.

16. On an overhead transparency, use a different colored highlighter to highlight each speaker's dialogue. Have students role-play the speakers' parts. Then, ask what they notice about the printed page that would help them detect the different speakers, like paragraphing and identifying the speaker by name.

17. The student will identify character traits through dialogue.

17. Take a familiar short story and rewrite a section of dialogue, but leave out the speaking verbs or attributes, such as "he said, she pleaded" or "they shouted." Let students substitute other verbs in the blanks and then justify their choices.

18. The student will identify characters through description.

18. Make an overhead transparency of a familiar short story. Color highlight the speaking verbs as well as additional descriptive phrases that indicate characters' facial expressions, physical actions or tone of voice. Repeat the activity with another story, allowing students to do the highlighting.

19. The student will recognize that stories can be told from different points of view.

19. Share with students different published versions of the same story, like a "fractured" fairy tale based on an original fairy tale. Or let students write their own versions of songs based on some original children's songs.

Individual Objectives	**Classroom Activities**
20. The student will compare and contrast people, things and ideas.	20. Use Venn diagrams frequently as you teach students the comprehension skills of comparing and contrasting. For example, after reading two similar short stories, have students compare and contrast the themes or ideas presented.
21. The student will read materials with various levels of sentence structure.	21. Encourage students to adapt their reading skills through exposure to a variety of materials, rather than material always controlled for simplicity of sentence structure or level of vocabulary skills. Students need to learn that true reading involves using a variety of strategies to make sense of words.
22. The student will vary reading rate according to the purpose of reading.	22. Have students scan a TV guide for the day and time of a favorite show. Then, have them read through a short description of a science experiment. Discuss in which case they needed to read more slowly and thoroughly and why.
23. The student will predict meanings of foreign-language words.	23. Read aloud a short story using foreign-language words, as your students read along from an overhead copy. Highlight the foreign-language words and discuss what students notice, like italics or an accent mark. Then, discuss what students do understand about the story and how they need not be able to translate exactly to understand the reading. Ask any students who know the language to explain the meaning.
24. The student will understand the purpose of variations in print, like all capitals or bold face.	24. Make a quick reference guide with examples of print variations and their purposes, like all capitals to show emphasis or strong emotion. Then, create a class story and have students use variations in print to enhance meaning.

52

Copyright © 1998 LinguiSystems, Inc.

Individual Objectives	**Classroom Activities**

25. The student will follow variations in reading formats, like captions and lists.

    25. Provide a variety of reading materials in your reading corner or library, like newspapers, telephone books, car manuals, or menus. Give students silent reading time to explore the different formats and then discuss their experiences with you. For new readers, use theme weeks to study different formats. For example, have students bring in recipes one week to read and maybe even experiment with cooking!

26. The student will use rereading to make sense of a reading passage.

    26. Divide a story into three or four logical divisions. After each section, ask students what they think is happening and what details seem to be important at that point. Continue to read the next section and follow with a similar discussion. Have they reconsidered what they thought at first? Why? Reread relevant passages to them to confirm their rethinking. Explain that any reader must reread certain passages in order to understand a story.

27. The student will use context clues to understand new words or phrases.

    27. Make an overhead transparency of a story containing four or five words likely to be familiar to your students and providing sufficient context to guess their meanings. Put blanks where the words belong. Let pairs of students predict words to fill the blanks, but do so independently. Then, have students share their guesses, pointing out context clues as well as their own experiences that helped confirm their predictions.

28. The student will understand and use survival words correctly in areas, like signs, cooking, restaurants, medicine, jobs, and driving.

    28. Teach theme units related to survival skills, emphasizing sight recognition of words and their practical meanings. Accompany units with real-life experiences, such as visiting a restaurant or the drivers' examination office.

53
Copyright © 1998 LinguiSystems, Inc.

Yearly Goal: to improve content area reading and comprehension

Content Area Reading

Individual Objectives

1. The student will understand the purpose of a table of contents, an index and a glossary.

2. The student will use the organization of a book for learning, like footnotes and appendices.

3. The student will learn to skim a content area reading assignment to discover its purpose.

4. The student will identify important information in individual content areas and their textbooks.

5. The student will take notes while reading.

Classroom Activities

1. Review the purposes of a table of contents (for broad categories of information), an index (for more specific information) and a glossary (to define individual words.) Then, have Information Hunts where teams of students are given "Where would you find . . . ?" types of questions and then must answer correctly. Extend the learning by using actual examples in students' textbooks.

2. After reading a passage, have students look up related information from footnotes or the appendices. Place questions on individual cards and assign students to find the information and then teach it to the rest of the students.

3. Have students create an idea web for the chapter. In the middle of the web, they write the title or main idea of the chapter. Then, students skim the chapter and add related ideas to the lines radiating from the title.

4. Knowing dates, places and people may be important in a history class, while understanding theories and principles may mean more in a science class. Read through a variety of assignments with students. Stop to discuss and underline or highlight, if possible, examples of what's important to know in each class and why.

5. Using bold titles and subtitles in a reading passage, have students make an outline of the main ideas and details. Later, have reading partners compare and improve their outlines. Encourage the students to use the outline to help find assignment answers.

Copyright © 1998 LinguiSystems, Inc.

Individual Objectives	**Classroom Activities**
6. The student will take notes while listening to a content-area lecture.	6. To help students organize what they hear, prepare listening guides prior to a lecture. The listening guide should include the main ideas of the lecture and its subtopics. As students listen, they fill in the details. Follow up with a discussion of how the lecture relates to reading they've done.
7. The student will interpret charts, maps and diagrams.	7. Before students read, have them skim the titles and captions used with any charts, maps or diagrams. Answer any questions they have about interpreting them. Then, as students read they can refer back to the charts, maps or diagrams to enhance their comprehension.
8. The student will identify and learn new vocabulary or concepts.	8. Before students read a chapter, have them make a three-column chart for new vocabulary words or concepts which are usually located at the beginning of the reading or as part of comprehension questions at the end. Have them write the vocabulary words or concepts in the first column, and then as they read, write the sentence(s) where each concept is discussed in the second column and its actual definition in the last column. In content-area reading, students must often read the sentences before and after where the word is located to understand it fully.
9. The student will recall main ideas from reading.	9. Break down content area reading into smaller chunks, assigning only major sections at a time. When students finish a section, they can summarize what they learned in a reading log.
10. The student will predict information to be covered in next reading section or chapter.	10. In groups, let students generalize the main points of what they just read. Then, have them formulate questions to be answered by material that logically would come next. Put the questions on the chalkboard or overhead projector and have students explain their thinking. As students continue to read and check their predictions, reward their accurate predictions.

Copyright © 1998 LinguiSystems, Inc.

Individual Objectives

Classroom Activities

11. The student will arrange events in sequential order, such as according to time, level of importance, or cause and effect.

11. Develop several organizers your students can choose to fill in as a way to summarize what they learn from their reading. In pairs, have students choose the appropriate organizer and fill it in.

    Examples:

What I learned about ____.	
First Event	
Second Event	
Third Event	

Causes of the ____.		
Cause	→	Effect
_____		_____
Cause	→	Effect
_____		_____
Cause	→	Effect
_____		_____

12. The student will use mnemonics to help memorize content-area concepts.

12. Demonstrate for your students a variety of ways to memorize material, such as putting dates and events to know in chronological order or memorizing the names of important scientists by making an association between their names and their discoveries. Students can devise their own study guides using mnemonics.

13. The student will read information from other sources, like the Internet, encyclopedias and almanacs.

13. Encourage students to brainstorm on paper several possible ways their topic might appear in a source. Then, review how to scan for key words while reading.

14. The student will apply word attack skills to content-area words.

14. Group new concepts and vocabulary by word features as you introduce them. For example, if you're studying various religions of the world, review the *-ism* and *-theism* suffixes appearing on words like *Buddhism, Catholicism, monotheism*, and *polytheism*.

Content Area Reading, *continued*

Individual Objectives	Classroom Activities
15. The student will read informational material for personal purposes.	15. Create a variety of scenarios when students might need to locate informational material, such as researching a state they might be visiting, or learning more about a disease that's been declared a national epidemic. Build time into the school day for frequent information searches. Make a bulletin board for students to share what they learn.
16. The student will summarize information from a nonfiction selection.	16. When students finish reading a nonfiction selection, have them write a paragraph in small groups. Each student should contribute sentences recalling important information to make the paragraph.

Yearly Goal: to build vocabulary skills

Vocabulary

1. The student will listen for context clues.	1. Use short rhymes and have students provide the words you leave out. Then, progress to books that repeat words and phrases often. Read a story through, then have students provide words as you read the story again.
2. The student will predict vocabulary to be used in a story.	2. Tap students' prior knowledge before reading. Introduce the subject of the story. Then, have students think of words associated with the subject. To reinforce vocabulary learning, have students make sentences using their words.
3. The student will fill in cloze procedure exercises.	3. Focus on only one aspect of using context clues at a time as you create 100-word passages. To enhance students' abilities to understand syntax clues, leave out words having -ing endings, for example. Or to enhance understanding main idea, leave out words related to the passage's subject.
4. The student will understand synonyms and antonyms.	4. To make synonym and antonym study fun, create student questionnaires to elicit their opinions on current topics. Have students express their opinions by choosing from a range of related vocabulary words, looking up words they don't know as they answer. (See the example on the next page.)

Copyright © 1998 LinguiSystems, Inc.

Individual Objectives

Classroom Activities

Example:
a. Some current dance moves are ____.
   complicated   facile

b. In the future, I'd like to live a ____ life.
   frugal   luxurious

c. When I'm stuck on an assignment, I ___.
   persevere with it   abandon it

5. The student will read and understand common homonyms, like *sea/see, blew/blue* and *whole/hole*.

5. Have students make picture cards to distinguish between each pair of homonyms. For example, the pair *sea/see* could be illustrated with a boat on the sea and a pair of eyes. Students can refer to the cards when figuring out word meaning or when they use the words in writing.

6. The student will learn how prefixes and suffixes affect word meanings.

6. Whenever students need to learn new words for a fiction or nonfiction reading selection, choose words with similar features, like prefixes and suffixes. Talk about word meanings with and without the prefixes and suffixes.

7. The student will learn to categorize words.

7. Whether you're sharing the day's school lunch menu or listing materials for a group project, share information with students by grouping it. Lunch menu items could include orange foods (macaroni and cheese, carrots and an orange) and white foods (mashed potatoes and milk). Discuss the features similar to each group and also suggest other ways to group items.

8. The student will identify the definitions of new words given within the context of the reading material.

8. Provide students with several examples demonstrating how the definition of a new word also follows its introduction in the reading. For example, an author may include the definition in parentheses or set off by commas in a separate phrase.

9. The student will choose the correct dictionary meaning to fit a word.

9. Provide new words within a context. Then, have students highlight surrounding words that can help them locate the word with the correct features.

Vocabulary, *continued*

Individual Objectives

10. The student will recognize root words in unknown words.

11. The student will recognize multiple meanings of words.

12. The student will use footnoted definitions or explanations.

13. The student will recognize common acronyms.

14. The student will use homophones appropriately.

15. The student will build vocabulary and interest in words.

Classroom Activities

10. Prefixes or suffixes generally add from two to five letters to a root word. On a list of new words with familiar roots, have students use a small slip of paper to cover up the first two or three letters. Ask if they recognize the root word. If not, follow the same procedure with the last three to five letters.

11. Have students make study guides of frequently read and used multiple-meaning words, like *tie, plain* and *scale*. Encourage students to illustrate or define each meaning. Leave room for students to add words as they learn more difficult words like *draft, relay* and *sentence*.

12. Provide students with a copy of a passage using several footnotes. Have them color highlight the word footnoted and its definition. Then, read the passage aloud and have students match the word with its definition.

13. Have students search for acronyms in current reading materials like newspapers and magazines. Create a bulletin board to post the acronyms and their meanings.

14. Students who understand homophones can usually use them appropriately when writing. Review common homophone problems, like *there, they're* and *their*, and help students develop their own memory tricks for distinguishing them. Then, dictate sentences with the homophones to give students practice in listening for context clues to help them decide which word to use.

15. Provide word games, crossword puzzles, riddles, and sayings for students to tackle during free time or while waiting after completing an assignment. Give rewards to students who solve tough challenges.

Copyright © 1998 LinguiSystems, Inc.

Writing

Grasping crayons with chubby three-year-old hands, your students begin to "write." First, they learn the strokes to write lines, then to print their names, and eventually to communicate basic thoughts and feelings in their first attempts at sentences. Teachers instruct them in good penmanship, spelling and grammar, rules for punctuation, and how to outline. Older students struggle to organize ideas into an essay and type it in polished form on the computer.

As you can see, writing is an extremely complex process, relying on the visual, auditory, motor, language, and thinking skills of the student. The objectives and classroom activities that follow will strengthen your students' skills in:

- Handwriting/Letter Formation
- Written Expression
- Writing Process
- Forms of Writing
- Word Processing
- Everyday Writing
- Capitalization and Punctuation
- Grammar
- Spelling

Copyright © 1998 LinguiSystems, Inc.

Writing

Yearly Goal: to learn and improve handwriting skills

Handwriting/Letter Formation

Individual Objectives

1. The student will learn the names of letters.

2. The student will recognize similarities and differences in shapes of letters.

3. The student will recognize similarities and differences in forming letters.

4. The student will recognize the space between written words.

5. The student will put appropriate space between words.

6. The student will hold a pen or pencil correctly.

Classroom Activities

1. Cut huge letters out of material like cardboard or outdoor carpeting. Allow students to walk around letters or feel letters like *L, C* and *S* to get a sense of directionality. Later, have students find pictures of words beginning with each letter and attach them to the letter.

2. Create a Concentration type game with letters. Have students place letter cards facedown and then turn cards over and make pairs from cards that are different (an *o* is round while a *z* is crooked) or alike (a *c* is round and an *o* is round). Or students can make pairs from letters that are identical. Color cue the shapes of letters as needed to help visual discrimination.

3. Model how to write two letters like an *l* and an *h*. Both have a straight line, but the *h* has an extra curved line. Have the student trace the similarities with one color and the differences with a different color.

4. Type simple sentences for students to read. As you read the sentences together, have students color with crayon or highlight marker the space that separates each word.

5. Teach students to use consistent spacing between words by providing a paper strip to place in between words as they write or having them use their index fingers.

6. Have students use pencil grips or thick pencils as needed. Model how to hold the pencil and write in the air with big movements to demonstrate. Then, have students write big on large pieces of paper. Use lines if needed.

Copyright © 1998 LinguiSystems, Inc.

Handwriting/Letter Formation, *continued*

Individual Objectives	**Classroom Activities**
7. The student will trace basic shapes and strokes of manuscript letters.	7. Use materials like sand, paint or sandpaper to help students feel the shapes of letters as they trace them.
8. The student will trace basic shapes and strokes of numbers.	8. Cut numbers out of materials like sandpaper, lightweight cardboard or foam rubber so students can feel the shapes or even trace around them to form numbers.
9. The student will identify the differences between capital and lower case manuscript letters.	9. Teach students when to use capital letters versus lower case letters. Explain that capital letters are bigger and shaped differently because "it's a BIG deal" when starting a sentence or writing someone's name.
10. The student will reproduce capital and lower case manuscript letters.	10. Have students stand and copy the letters in the air. Have them use large motions for each capital letter and smaller motions for lower case letters.
11. The student will write letters from the alphabet in manuscript from memory.	11. Have the student learn auditory cues related to the shapes of the letters to help them memorize. For example, an *a* is a round line with a tail, a *b* is a straight line with a round line and a *c* is a round, open line. Students should repeat the cues as they write.
12. The student will stay on the line while writing.	12. Tape the top corners of students' papers to their desks to anchor their papers and facilitate copying.
13. The student will copy in manuscript in the correct space on a piece of paper.	13. To help students with directionality problems, place a colored line down the left side of the page to indicate where they should begin writing and a different colored line on the right to show where to stop.
14. The student will copy words or simple sentences from the chalkboard in manuscript.	14. As an intermediate step to copying on their own papers, allow students to copy using an overhead projector. Write a sentence on the overhead. Then, have a student copy the same sentence right below it on a line provided. Have the student check his work.

Handwriting/Letter Formation, *continued*

Individual Objectives

15. The student will write letters or words in manuscript as dictated by the teacher.

16. The student will write sentences of his own in manuscript.

Note: For cursive writing, apply the same gradual steps used in the goals for manuscript writing as above, but with emphasis on writing strokes and connecting letters to form words.

Classroom Activities

15. Dictate letters or words into a tape recorder. Let students monitor the pace at which they write by pausing the tape recorder as needed.

16. Real writing occurs when students write to communicate ideas. Provide pictures for students to write stories about. Let students write their stories on paper with fun borders.

Yearly Goal: to organize and express ideas through writing

Written Expression ....

1. The student will use labels or captions to express ideas.

2. The student will use noun and verb clauses relevant to the topic.

3. The student will explain ideas using clear descriptions.

1. Encourage early writing by having students label or caption things they illustrate as part of classroom activities. Allow inventive spelling or have students dictate their ideas.

2. As students move beyond labeling and captioning, they may attempt to write complete sentences. After classroom activities, frequently let students dictate language experience stories to you. Write exactly what students say and read their sentences back to them, highlighting nouns and verbs. You can call the words *People, Place, Thing* (nouns) or *Action Words* (verbs) so students learn the basics of sentence writing.

3. Model clear description for your students. When you return from an experience, like supervising the playground, tell students what you saw, heard and felt. Encourage them to elaborate upon their experiences on a frequent basis, too.

Copyright © 1998 LinguiSystems, Inc.

Written Expression, *continued*

Individual Objectives	Classroom Activities
4. The student will write two or more sentences on a topic.	4. Give students many opportunities to reflect on past experiences. Before reading a story, have students write sentences about experiences similar to what they'll read about. Continue to allow students to dictate as needed.
5. The student will express ideas in grammatically complete sentences.	5. Give students a formula to follow for writing a complete sentence.
6. The student will expand basic sentences using describing words.	6. Provide pictures of objects, animals or people. Then, provide a list of questions to refer to, such as "What does it look like? What does it sound like?" and "What does it smell like?" to prompt more description of the nouns. Let students write sentences about the pictures and then compare what they write.
7. The student will choose appropriate words to convey intended meaning.	7. Cut out magazine pictures showing active scenes and a lot of description. Then, write two sentences for each picture, one conveying a description of the picture more specifically and logically than the other. Have students choose the most appropriate sentence. Then, have students choose pictures and write sentences of their own.
8. The student will sequence ideas in an order appropriate to the topic.	8. Dictate related sentences to your students as they write them on strips of paper. Practice with sentences that have a chronological order, like in retelling a story, or a logical order of their own. Then, have students work in pairs to decide on the correct order of sentences. Discuss how related sentences form paragraphs.

Noun (Who?)	Verb (Did What?)	Noun (to What or Whom?)
The librarian	checked out	the book.

Copyright © 1998 LinguiSystems, Inc.

Written Expression, *continued*

Individual Objectives	Classroom Activities
9. The student will write sentences of varied complexity.	9. Have students do exercises on combining sentences. Provide a reference list of connecting words like conjunctions or prepositions. Encourage students to rearrange the order of words, too.
10. The student will write sentences of varied styles.	10. Keep a portfolio of each student's writing. Look over several samples of the writing with the student to note any patterns. For example, the student may begin every sentence with *There, Then* or *Because*. Put together an individualized reference guide for the student with different ways to express the same ideas.
11. The student will stick with ideas relevant to the topic.	11. Compare checking for relevant information to sticking with a conversation or discussion topic. As part of revision, have students read their writing and highlight sentences that stick to the topic. Let them omit or revise sentences that are irrelevant.
12. The student will generate ideas for writing.	12. Provide a variety of oral or written activities during which students practice skills like brainstorming, clustering and semantic mapping. Tie experiences into other curricular classes or school experiences like field trips.
13. The student will make a simple outline.	13. While generating ideas for a topic, write related ideas on index cards, one idea per card. With the student, put together related ideas. Finally, number and letter the idea cards and arrange them in the form of an outline.
14. The student will write a cohesive paragraph.	14. Have students practice thinking of ideas associated with a topic. Provide slips of paper with familiar topics written on them. Each student chooses a topic and brainstorms ideas. Then, the student can dictate the sentences into a tape recorder, to a partner or to the teacher who helps shape the ideas into connected sentences.

Copyright © 1998 LinguiSystems, Inc.

Written Expression, *continued*

Individual Objectives	Classroom Activities
15. The student will write paragraphs from an outline.	15. Have each student write an outline on paper, leaving several spaces between numbered or lettered items so the outline acts as a skeleton for writing. Each student then writes a sentence related to each item below it. Paragraphs can later be rewritten without the outlines.
16. The student will use writing as a learning tool.	16. Using writing frequently in your class helps students view writing as an integral part of the learning process. As lead-ins to class discussions, have students write their ideas on a key question. Or after a new concept has been taught, have students journal write about what they've learned.

Writing Process

1. The student will vary word and sentence choices to fit audience and purpose.	1. Choose a topic and have students write two different versions, one for adults and one for students younger than them. Then, have students analyze the differences in word and sentence choices due to a change in audience.
2. The student will learn the steps in the writing process.	2. Have students make individual posters to use at their desks to remind them of the writing process — brainstorming, writing, revising, proofreading, and publishing. When making writing assignments, ask to see proof of students using the steps, like brainstorming, rough drafts and use of proofreading symbols, and evaluate students on completeness of the steps.
3. The student will revise what's been written to clarify ideas.	3. Anytime a student is asked to revise, provide a narrow focus about what should be looked at. For example, if a student has been asked to write a narrative, the focus could be on including all the story details or using dialogue appropriately.

Copyright © 1998 LinguiSystems, Inc.

Individual Objectives	**Classroom Activities**
4. The student will learn proofreading techniques.	4. Students should have a reference guide with common proofreading symbols. Provide exercises where students use the symbols to improve writing. Have students skip lines when they write to allow room for proof-reading marks and corrections.
5. The student will make writing presentable for publication.	5. Have students frequently share their writing with people outside the classroom before they publish it. Arrange for a group of school personnel to be writing partners for students. They can read the work back to the student and ask key questions that help students improve their writing.
6. The student will think and write creatively.	6. In class discussions, frequently ask "What would happen if . . . ?" and "Why do you think . . . ?" types of questions. Make posters and drawings of your students' wildest thoughts to encourage creative and divergent thinking.

Forms of Writing

1. The student will write a tall tale.	1. As a lead-in or brainstorming activity, let students practice telling tall tales about things that have happened to them or provide them with story starters. Let them exaggerate and stretch the truth in fun ways by asking questions that encourage them to add description and details, like "How big was the . . .?" or "How strong was the . . .?" Tape record your students' tales for future classes.
2. The student will write a folktale.	2. Combine studying a science theme, like the stars and the sky, with an exploration of folktales. Include reading folktales about things like how the constellations began or the discovery of shooting stars. Then, let students make up picture folktales to illustrate their own theories about astrological events.

Copyright © 1998 LinguiSystems, Inc.

Forms of Writing, *continued*

Individual Objectives	Classroom Activities
3. The student will write a book review.	3. After reading a short story or novel with your students, write a class review. Demonstrate what to include, like characters, plot summary and an evaluation of the work. Write a draft on an overhead projector transparency and then review it for content and quality of writing. Type up the review and have students add a cover or other illustrations to the work to make it publishable.
4. The student will write an opinion paper.	4. Bring in editorial pages from newspapers or magazines. Have students use a color highlighter to highlight the opinion statement in an editorial in one color and then the reasons offered by the author in another color. Let students write dissenting opinions justified with their own reasons.
5. The student will develop a paragraph in different ways, for example with details, reasons or examples.	5. Provide real-life examples of paragraphs from newspaper or magazine articles. Have students locate the topic sentence and then highlight the details, reasons or examples used to develop it.
6. The student will plan and answer essay questions in paragraph form.	6. Before tests, have curricular area teachers provide possible topics for essays or even sample essay questions. Have students research information and write model answers. Let partners check for completeness of paragraphs.
7. The student will write a complete essay including an introduction, body and conclusion.	7. Make a visual reminder of the structure of an essay so students remember to include all parts. A "sandwich" like the one below could be used for brainstorming as an overhead transparency or as an individual student activity sheet.

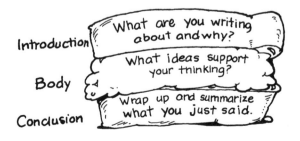

Introduction — What are you writing about and why?

Body — What ideas support your thinking?

Conclusion — Wrap up and summarize what you just said.

Copyright © 1998 LinguiSystems, Inc.

Forms of Writing, *continued*

Individual Objectives

8. The student will locate and use resources for research.

9. The student will summarize and take notes for a research paper.

10. The student will write a comparison and contrast paper.

11. The student will express personal feelings through writing.

12. The student will write a narrative.

Classroom Activities

8. Create Knowledge Chaser games. Any time you or another teacher begins a new unit, send students to the library or media center to research concepts ahead of time. As you introduce the new concepts, students can share what they learned and where they got their information.

9. Help students create an advanced organizer for their research. Predict categories of information they might locate on their topic and label large individual index cards with them. As students read and take notes, they put the information under the correct category.

10. Use a three-column chart labeled *Alike, Different* and *True for Both* to help students brainstorm ideas. Do several brainstorming examples with the class ranging from concrete things like places and objects, to more abstract things like people's personalities or current musical trends. Then, have students write papers, providing them with a list of transitional phrases like *also, both, alike, similar, opposite,* and *different* to help them express their ideas.

11. In anticipation of a special event at school or to help students adjust to a new situation, have students react to "I feel . . ." statements and explain their reasons.

    After the event or situation, have students review their earlier writing and react to how they feel now.

12. Have students bring in favorite photos from a birthday, vacation or other event. First, have them write captions to go with the pictures. Then, have students elaborate on what's happening from one picture to the next in the correct order. Encourage students to write dialogue if they know how.

Copyright © 1998 LinguiSystems, Inc.

Forms of Writing, *continued*

Individual Objectives	Classroom Activities
13. The student will explain in writing how to do something.	13. Have students think of a place they know how to get to or a thing they can do well. Next, have students list each step separately on a slip of paper or an index card so they can rearrange the order as needed. Then, put the slips in random order and have another student familiar with the place or process arrange the slips and steps. Students should discuss any discrepancies in order or missing information.
14. The student will write a descriptive passage.	14. "Time travel" with your students to their earlier years to recall vivid memories. With the lights low or off and the room quiet, ask your students to go back to their scariest experience and recall what they saw, heard, felt, tasted, or smelled. Then, ask them to go back to their happiest experience. Turn the lights back on and have students elaborate on one of these experiences in a journal entry.
15. The student will write a persuasive passage.	15. Have frequent "convince me" discussions so students practice reasoning skills. Lead in to discussions with statements related to current topics studied. For example, you could use a lead-in statement, such as "Convince me that democracy is the best form of government" or "Convince me that smoking should not be allowed in public places." Have students summarize the discussion later in their journals.
16. The student will write a friendly letter.	16. Have school personnel, like the principal or a cafeteria worker, write friendly letters to your students. Letters might comment on a class project, invite them to visit the office or praise appropriate behavior in the lunch line. Let students decide from reading the letter models what a friendly letter should include and then write letters in response.

Copyright © 1998 LinguiSystems, Inc.

Forms of Writing, *continued*

Individual Objectives

17. The student will write a business letter.

18. The student will write an autobiography.

19. The student will write a character analysis.

20. The student will write a resume.

Classroom Activities

17. Provide a partially written letter model for students to fill in the blanks with information about a certain business. For example, all students might write letters about their favorite snacks or candy and request samples. Students would fill in the company name, the snack name and their opinion. Then, students can use what they've learned when they receive their samples as they write follow-up thank-you business letters.

18. As part of brainstorming for the autobiography, have a parent or guardian list details they remember about the child and include any favorite photos. Students can then add their own ideas and memories and expand them into an autobiography complete with illustrations and captions.

19. Initially, when teaching students to analyze characters, have them read a book in which the character presentations are fairly consistent between the book and a video presentation of the book. Have students write their first drafts after reading the book. Then, have students revise their papers after the video where the characters are perhaps presented more dynamically.

20. Students as young as fourth and fifth grade can begin to create personal data sheets or resumes to include as part of their IEP folders. School personnel will learn more about them and students may also link current coursework and activities to their future goals.

Copyright © 1998 LinguiSystems, Inc.

Word Processing

Individual Objectives

1. The student will learn the layout of the keyboard.

2. The student will accurately copy sentences using the keyboard.

3. The student will learn a word processing program.

4. The student will learn to use computer tools for checking spelling.

5. The student must proof written work using the computer.

6. The student will use a text-to-speech program like SimpleText® to generate and proof written work.

7. The student will learn to edit using a word-processing program.

Classroom Activities

1. Provide a true-to-size diagram of the keyboard and have the student practice positioning her hands. Dictate progressing from simple words to short sentences so students get used to where letters are located.

2. Let students copy isolated sentences written on strips and taped on the edge of the monitor or stand. After copying each sentence correctly including punctuation and capitalization two or three times, have students choose another strip to copy. Incorporate spelling practice in the sentences as a bonus.

3. Use a typing program from any company that begins with one-sentence practice exercises. Encourage students to look over their work after each sentence they type.

4. Make a study guide or poster explaining and illustrating the step-by-step instructions for checking spelling on the computer. Have students purposely misspell a few words to get practice using the spell checker.

5. Incorporate computer proofreading into your grading system or assignment expectations. Have students print a "before" and "after" copy of their writing to document their work.

6. When students first learn to use the program, let them play around with the various voice choices as well as with what they write. Then, have them write very short paragraphs. Encourage students to highlight and listen to one sentence of the paragraph at a time as they check their writing.

7. Give students short stories on computer with passages that are out of order or sentences that are incomplete. Have students check for completion and sequence of ideas. Then, they can use the cut, paste and copy functions to move text and clarify ideas.

Word Processing, *continued*

Individual Objectives	Classroom Activities
8. The student will use the computer to take classroom notes.	8. Provide tape recorded notes to simulate a classroom situation. Students can start and stop the tape as they get used to translating what they hear to what they type.

Everyday Writing

Individual Objectives	Classroom Activities
1. The student will write his own name and address.	1. Let students "mail" their assignments to you. Provide envelopes, "stamps" and your address. Students then have to write their return addresses in the proper place before turning in assignments.
2. The student will learn common abbreviations.	2. Bring in resources like newspapers, calendars and measurement tables. Compile and group lists of common abbreviations students might use as they write personal notes, take class notes or complete projects at home.
3. The student will take an accurate message.	3. Tape record a variety of situations for students to practice taking messages. For example, students may need to take phone messages at home, deliver a message to a neighbor, or take a message from a customer to an employer. Discuss the importance of the content and timing of the delivery of the message.
4. The student will write a thank-you note.	4. Have students brainstorm what someone has done for them lately. Then, have students write and deliver thank-you notes.
5. The student will write a to-do list.	5. As a matter of routine, have students write to-do lists to plan their evenings. Have them return the lists the next day with items crossed off that they accomplished.
6. The student will write a friendly letter.	6. Set up Letter Buddies with another class. Have students write friendly letters frequently to get to know their buddies.

Copyright © 1998 LinguiSystems, Inc.

Individual Objectives	**Classroom Activities**
7. The student will write a business letter.	7. Set up a business partnership ahead of time with a local business. Have students write letters to ask questions about the business and eventually to request a tour. After the tour, students can write letters sharing what they learned as well as thanking the business.
8. The student will write a resume.	8. Provide a variety of resume examples, especially where things like school activities and volunteer experiences count toward job experience. Make sure students produce word-processed professional-looking resumes.
9. The student will complete a job application.	9. Based on samples of job applications, have each student make up a job application form for a future career. The student should tailor the job application to the type of information important to the job, as well as including standard job application information. Encourage the student to type the form and then complete it.
10. The student will explore ways writing will be used in a future career.	10. Students can practice interviewing skills and learn about future job writing demands by interviewing local employers. Students should take notes or tape record answers. Then, have them evaluate the appropriateness of their writing skills to the job.

Capitalization and Punctuation ....

1. The student will recognize the main idea of a sentence.	1. Students who don't punctuate well often don't recognize the main idea or subject of a sentence and consequently don't recognize when writing shifts subtly from one idea to another to indicate a new sentence. Write a series of two to three simple, related sentences without punctuation on the chalkboard. Read the entire set aloud. Then, ask "What two to three ideas are being talked about here?" As students name each one, capitalize and then punctuate the start and end of each main idea sentence.

Capitalization and Punctuation, *continued*

Individual Objectives

2. The student will recognize the beginning and end of a sentence.

3. The student will identify and punctuate different types of sentences.

4. The student will write and punctuate abbreviations correctly.

5. The student will learn why words are capitalized.

6. The student will use capital letters in written work.

Classroom Activities

2. Read sets of two to three short sentences to your students. When students hear what they think is the end of a sentence, ask them to clap their hands. Discuss what made one sentence separate from the other.

3. Make wacky face signs for students to hold up as they practice distinguishing between a question, a statement, an exclamation, or a command. For example, the question mark face can show someone with a puzzled look or the command look can show someone pointing as if he's directing someone to do something. Include the punctuation mark on the face sign, too. Then, write and read aloud unpunctuated sentences on the chalkboard and have students hold up the appropriate face for each sentence.

4. Have students come up with examples of abbreviations they use every day like *hr., min., Mon., Tues., mi., ft., Mr., Mrs.,* and *Dr.* Then, dictate fun sentences to students in which they translate what they hear into abbreviations, such as "Mrs. Rose became Dr. Rose after she went to school for eight yrs., six mos. and forty-nine hrs." Have teams of students compete to find all the words that can be abbreviated.

5. Explain that capital letters are used to make words or groups of words special, like for holiday names, names of people and places, and for book titles. Then, spend several days compiling lists on a poster of days, people, places, books, and so on related to school or having special meaning in your students' lives and experiences.

6. Provide a capitalization study guide listing the rules you expect students to learn at their particular grade level. Personalize the guide by illustrating rules with examples related to the student, to other students and to events at school.

Capitalization and Punctuation, *continued*

Individual Objectives	Classroom Activities
7. The student will use quotation marks appropriately.	7. Spend time exposing students to the use of quotation marks in a variety of types of reading, like newspaper stories and short stories. Have students try to identify some of the rules for quotations, such as indenting before each new speaker or using quotes before and after what someone says. Write their ideas on the chalkboard or overhead projector. Then, make a poster of quotation rules for student reference using their ideas.
8. The student will learn to use the comma in letter and envelope parts.	8. As students read stories, have them write letters to favorite characters. Let them make up addresses to include on the letters and envelopes. Then, write and actually mail letters to the students at their own addresses as if you were the character.
9. The student will learn to use the comma in a list or series of items.	9. Let students have fun punctuating sentences that include series of related items, such as "The things that bug me most are nosy sisters, gum in my hair, and having to eat school lunch." Have students generate a lot of lists and turn them into sentences.
10. The student will use the comma to make writing clearer.	10. Commas are frequently used to make complex sentences with phrases and clauses clearer. As your students' writing progresses and you see evidence of appositives, introductory phrases and clauses being used, provide individualized mini-lessons in using commas to punctuate them.
11. The student will use an apostrophe to write contractions and possessives.	11. Make individual reference cards students can tape to their desks. Include frequently used contractions as well as examples of correct use of apostrophes in possessives. Use a highlight color to emphasize placement of the apostrophe.
12. The student will learn to hyphenate words in writing.	12. Practice listening skills by having students listen for syllables in words. Using reading, spelling, vocabulary, or curricular words currently studied, read words one by one as students write them and then divide them into syllables.

Copyright © 1998 LinguiSystems, Inc.

Grammar

Individual Objectives

1. The student can distinguish between naming (nouns) and action (verbs) words.

2. The student will use singular or plural noun forms correctly.

3. The student will use correct subject and verb agreement in writing.

4. The student will use appropriate past, present and future verb tenses.

5. The student will form possessives correctly.

6. The student will use pronouns appropriately in writing.

Classroom Activities

1. Bring in common objects that are easy to name and demonstrate their actions. Write sentences about the objects on the chalkboard and have students act them out, such as "The plane flies," "The pencil writes," and "The girls shake hands."

2. Create lotto cards with pictures and words of things that form their singulars and plurals in similar ways. For example, for *dogs* and *zebras*, simply add *-s* for a plural, while for *tomatoes* and *lunches*, add *-es* for a plural. Students make matches by putting together similar noun forms.

3. As students write, have them skip lines between separate sentences. Then, partners can read back each sentence to the writer, focusing on subject and verb agreement.

4. Have students write short paragraphs about something they did today. Students should underline verbs and check them for use of correct present tense. Then, have students exchange papers and rewrite the paragraph using past tense and then future tense, again underlining the verb changes. Encourage them to look for patterns in endings.

5. Watch a short video of an athletic event where students are familiar with the players and sport. Have students make up sentences about the event using possessives, such as "Michael Jordan's rebound record improved tonight."

6. Provide paragraphs for students to insert pronouns. Students read the paragraphs with specific nouns first. Help students underline the nouns as they read. Then, provide small strips of paper with individual pronouns on them. Students glue or tape the pronoun over the noun it replaces. Discuss how interchanging nouns and pronouns helps writing sound smooth.

Copyright © 1998 LinguiSystems, Inc.

Individual Objectives

7. The student will recognize and use complete sentences.

8. The student will use irregular forms of verbs correctly.

9. The student will use adjectives and adverbs to create complex sentences.

10. The student will learn the correct use of commonly confused words like *to, two, too* and *there, their, they're*.

Classroom Activities

7. Play a game of Sentence Add-ons between teams of students. Write sentences and sentence fragments on strips of overhead transparency or on the chalkboard. Then, let students go to the board or overhead and correctly punctuate the sentence or complete the fragment to make a sentence. If the team is incorrect, another team can fix the sentence.

8. Make audiotapes for students to listen to. Students listen to sentences using irregular forms correctly, such as "Ben saw a killer whale at Sea World" or incorrectly, such as "I seen a fire last night." Students can use a thumbs-up sign for correct usage and a thumbs-down sign for errors.

9. Make sentence expansion cards. Create a variety of noun and verb cards as well as adverbs and adjectives. Have students put together cards to make sentences ranging in complexity from a simple N-V sentence like "The cat purred" to a complex N-V-N-Adv sentence like "Renee finished the test quickly." Color code cards, like making all nouns yellow, to make selection easier.

10. Though homophones are often addressed as a vocabulary or spelling issue, the problem really lies in students choosing the correct word based on its function in a sentence. Have students make reference guides or cards that show the word used correctly in a sentence. Then, make fill-in-the blank sentences for students to practice inserting the correct word.

Spelling ....

1. The student will write letters of the alphabet in capital and lower case.

1. Play a game of Capital Letter or Little Letter. Review why certain words get capitals. Then, as you say a word, the student writes or traces in the air a capital letter or a lower case letter.

Copyright © 1998 LinguiSystems, Inc.

Individual Objectives	**Classroom Activities**
2. The student will recognize the sounds made by individual letters.	2. With your students, create a multimedia program for bombarding students simultaneously with the sound and look of a letter. Videotape students holding letter cards and saying sounds with word examples. Include pause time in the tape so students watching later can repeat aloud and trace letter shapes in the air as practice.
3. The student will discriminate between letter sounds.	3. Create Alphabet Bingo cards for consonants and later for vowels. Read familiar words to your students, having them identify the beginning sound and covering that letter on the card. For vowels, read consonant-vowel-consonant pattern words like *pot* and *mess*, and have students cover the correct medial vowel sound.
4. The student will visually recognize words beginning with certain letters.	4. Make class alphabet lists using words of importance to your students like their names, their favorite activities or familiar places or things. For example, the B list could include *Barry, baseball* and *Bookmobile.*
5. The student will recognize that sounds or phonemes are made by groups of letters.	5. When teaching students to recognize how groups of letters can make one sound, use the squares in graph paper to "hold" the sounds. For example, the word *phone* would take up three sound squares. 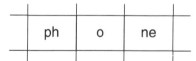
6. The student will learn common vowel sounds and vowel combinations.	6. Provide a list of words within the student's functional reading and spelling level that illustrates each vowel sound. Allow students to refer to the list when they do written work. Be sure to include words that are exceptions to rules, too, so students use visual memory as well as phonetics in spelling and reading.
7. The student will learn consonant blends and consonant pairs.	7. Have auditory training sessions. Provide flash cards with consonant blends and digraphs on them. As you say certain words, students hold up the correct flash card. For example, a session could focus on blends at the beginning of words like *bl* or *st.*

Individual Objectives	**Classroom Activities**
8. The student will learn to spell common word prefixes and suffixes.	8. Review how prefixes and suffixes change the meaning of a word when they're added to it. Then, have students learn the spelling and meanings of groups of related words like *impossible* and *improper*.
9. The student will learn to spell root words and other words derived from them.	9. Play chalkboard games where you write a root like *build*. Then, students compete to make new words from the root like *building, builder* and *rebuild*. As they write new word forms, they must also provide their meanings.
10. The student will improve visual memory for words.	10. Before students attempt any spelling lists, make sure they've heard and seen the words frequently. Make up or read stories using the words or use words from language experience stories the class writes.
11. The student will improve visual closure skills.	11. Checking spelling or proofreading requires students to have a sense of how long a word should be and what it should look like. Play games with students like Hangman or write short sentences, leaving letters out of common words.
12. The student will increase awareness of letter and sound relationships.	12. Label things around the room to increase visual memory. Have students make up sentences and rhymes about the items and tape record what they say. For example, students might say "The ball is near the wall" or "The bear is sitting on the chair." Note similarities as well as differences in sound representations.
13. The student will write simple sentences using correct spelling.	13. Challenge students to rack up "correct sentence" records. When a student correctly writes a sentence, he can add a tally mark or other symbol to a chart. Keep the chart for the year so the student can see growth from one week to the next. Reward students for every ten correct sentences, or so. Increase the "value" of a sentence as level of words or complexity of structure increases.

Copyright © 1998 LinguiSystems, Inc.

Spelling, *continued*

Individual Objectives	Classroom Activities
14. The student will spell frequently-used words.	14. Make and play lotto games with frequently-used words like *the, they, was,* and *because.* As students match pairs of words, they must say the word and spell it aloud.
15. The student will learn standard rules for spelling.	15. Using words within students' functional spelling level, teach students the basic phonetic rules like the phoneme /k/ which stands for *k, c* or *ck.* Also teach rules based on morphemes or small meaningful language units like *-ing* endings on verbs and adding *-es* or *-s* for plurals. Have students make spelling "dictionaries" highlighting a rule. Students could write sentences using the words and then illustrate the plurals, for example.
16. The student will use visual strategies to recognize spelling patterns in words.	16. Collect class lists of words with similar spelling patterns, like *look, book, mood,* and *blood.* Discuss how the words are pronounced and then group them on study guide sheets by sound patterns.
17. The student will use any punctuation correctly in spelling, like the period or apostrophe.	17. Include words with apostrophes or abbreviations as part of any spelling instruction, especially of frequently-used words. Students need to know that all aspects of the word are necessary to make a word "look" and be spelled right.
18. The student will strengthen visual memory for spelling.	18. Write each new word to learn individually on the overhead projector. Highlight in color certain features of the word to notice closely. Then, "roll" the word out of the line of vision and have students recall the word and its distinct features. Repeat often until the word is mastered. Go on to the next word, but review previous words as you progress to reinforce their visual memory.

Copyright © 1998 LinguiSystems, Inc.

Spelling, *continued*

Individual Objectives	Classroom Activities
19. The student will develop an effective, individual method for learning to spell words.	19. Create a spelling folder for each student. As you notice patterns of misspelling in your students' written work, record the words they need to learn. Then, have students decide what learning method works best for them, such as spelling aloud, tracing words, writing them large on the chalkboard, or just looking at them as they work on a few words at a time.
20. The student will check own written work for correct spelling.	20. Have students circle or highlight words they suspect are misspelled. Then, provide a variety of resources for the students to double-check their work, like a proofing partner, a dictionary or a spell checker on computer.
21. The student will write more frequently to practice spelling.	21. Create a lot of practical and fun ways to practice spelling. Dictate silly sentences and stories on audiotape for students to transcribe. Or have days when only writing and no talking is allowed. For example, a student has to write a request to borrow a pencil or word a question to ask for help.
22. The student will use other resources to ensure correct spelling.	22. As often as possible, build in time for students to use dictionaries or put assignments on computer and check their writing for spelling accuracy. Encourage students to look for patterns in the kinds of words they miss and record these words on individual lists for future study.
23. The student will learn to spell regular plurals of words.	23. Train students to discriminate the difference between the *-s* on the end of some plurals and the *-es* on the ends of others. Make individual *-s* and *-es* index cards for students. Then, read off a list of words like *books, chairs, matches,* and *wishes*. After each word, students hold up the correct plural card. Confirm their answers by spelling each word correctly on the board. Help students eventually make the generalization that words ending in *-ch* or *-sh* make plurals by adding *-es*.

Individual Objectives	Classroom Activities
24. The student will learn to spell irregular plurals of words.	24. Make a poster of Puzzling Plurals for words like *deer, geese* and *calves* so students understand the need to visually memorize confusing or puzzling plural forms.
25. The student will spell "spelling demons" or commonly misspelled words.	25. Try to group instruction by some common feature of the spelling demons. For example, the words *since, silence, piece*, and *practice* all end in *-ce* and the words *there's* and *here's* are contractions.
26. The student will learn to spell compound words.	26. Study words in compound word groups based on the same word like *father, stepfather, grandfather,* and *father-in-law*. Have students make up sentences illustrating the changes in meaning of each compound.
27. The student will learn spelling rules for common verb endings.	27. Combine teaching the grammatical use of verbs with spelling patterns. For example, a word with a short vowel like *stop* doubles the last letter before adding a new verb ending (*stopping*). Have students make lists of verbs in a variety of tenses and then look for generalizations and patterns.
28. The student will expand spelling vocabulary.	28. Incorporate vocabulary improvement as an aspect of students' spelling programs. For example, teach a list incorporating antonyms and synonyms like *loss* and *defeat, shiny* and *bright,* or *quiet* and *noisy*.

Copyright © 1998 LinguiSystems, Inc.

Literary Concepts

Cradled in the crook of your mom or dad's arm, you sat entranced by the words of your favorite book being read aloud to you. Imaginary people and characters came alive, if only for a few minutes. And when your mom or dad finished reading, you begged, "Please read it again" and they began again for the hundredth time.

Like you, your students enjoy hearing a good story conveyed by well chosen words. More importantly, though, they benefit from the models of human behavior portrayed in stories. Students learn about and rehearse social skills within the safe environment created by imaginary characters and situations. And, they rehearse how to think through situations in their own lives because they've observed and learned from characters' successes and failures.

The objectives and activities that follow will provide your students with experiences to develop social, language and thinking skills through literature as they learn about:

- Characterization
- Plot, Setting, Conflict
- Literary Techniques
- Figurative Language
- Fiction
- Nonfiction

Literary Concepts

Yearly Goal: to understand and apply the elements of literature

Characterization ··

Individual Objectives

1. The student will interpret pictures as they relate to the story.

2. The student will describe characters in a story.

3. The student will understand the role of dialogue in storytelling.

4. The student will analyze dialogue to understand a character.

5. The student will understand motives for a character's behaviors.

Classroom Activities

1. Have students read plenty of picture books. After reading a book, cover up the text and have students make up and write picture dialogues.

2. Using photographs and pictures of real and imaginary characters, have students brainstorm describing words to suit each character's looks and personality. Include famous people like Martin Luther King, Ryne Sandberg or Hillary Rodham Clinton as characters, as well as famous people from your own school like the librarian, a favorite teacher or a coach.

3. Provide students with puppets and allow them to make up a story line. Write their actions and dialogue in story form to reread. Later, discuss what students learn about the puppet characters from their dialogue and actions.

4. Color highlight phrases in dialogue that help describe a character. Have students list traits suggested by the dialogue.

5. Once you've read enough of a story, list the main characters and their traits on the chalkboard. Then, each time you read about an event in which the character reacts, stop to ask why the character just acted as he did. Have students compare the character's reaction to what they might have done.

Copyright © 1998 LinguiSystems, Inc.

Characterization, *continued*

Individual Objectives

6. The student will identify how a character has changed in a story.

Classroom Activities

6. Read a story about a character who goes through a significant life change or who learns an important lesson. Have students make a chart labeled *Before* and *After*. Then, have students fill in the character's traits before the major event and then his new traits after the event.

   For older students, have them consider if the changes are for the better. Introduce the terms *static* (no change) and *dynamic* (changed) to describe characters if students are ready for the concepts.

Plot, Setting, Conflict

1. The student will determine important details in a story.

1. Before students can understand important literary terms, like *setting* and *character*, they need to recognize the important five W's of a story — *Who, What, Where, When,* and *Why.* After reading a relatively short story, make a five-column chart labeled with the five W's. One at a time, brainstorm details for each W. Then, yay or nay each detail by either keeping it or drawing a line through it based on its importance to the story.

2. The student will complete a story map.

2. Provide students with a graphic organizer for story mapping. Fill out examples together as you read before students read a story and complete one independently.

3. The student will retell the plot of a story or chapter.

3. To help students recall events from the story, prepare a hint sheet ahead of time. On the hint sheet, include key ideas or phrases from the reading. In pairs, one student summarizes events while the other student checks off the related phrase or key word. Students then exchange roles to complete the task.

Copyright © 1998 LinguiSystems, Inc.

Plot, Setting, Conflict, *continued*

Individual Objectives	**Classroom Activities**

4. The student will predict what will happen next in a story.

4. To encourage active listening, copy key predictable paragraphs from the reading selection. Have students read the paragraphs and guess how the information might fit into the story. Then, read aloud to students pausing in the predictable places. Have students decide which paragraph completes the prediction.

5. The student will correctly sequence the events in a story.

5. Using paper or strips of overhead transparency, create sentence summary strips of key events from the story you're about to read. Give each student a strip to read aloud. After hearing the story, students then work together to put the strips in the correct order.

6. The student will understand the four types of conflict in a story.

6. Apply the concept of conflict to real-life. List on the chalkboard student examples from everyday life that illustrate struggles or needs to work things out. Apply the labels *man vs. man*, *man vs. nature*, *man vs. self*, and *man vs. fate* to their examples.

   man vs. man — getting through the lunch line quickly
   man vs. self — remembering to do my homework
   man vs. nature — soccer practice cancelled due to rain
   man vs. fate — finding $20 on the sidewalk

7. The student will identify and label the type of conflict in a story.

7. Read a story with one or two clear conflicts. Begin by reading far enough to identify the major characters in the story and discuss what they're like. Then, read until you get to the first conflict. Have students tell who or what is involved in the conflict and also identify the type of conflict. Let students predict how the conflict might turn out. Continue reading to identify any other conflicts as well as to confirm their predictions.

Copyright © 1998 LinguiSystems, Inc.

Plot, Setting, Conflict, *continued*

Individual Objectives

8. The student will identify the climax of a story.

9. The student will identify the resolution of a story.

10. The student will understand and apply the elements of a plot line.

11. The student will learn vocabulary relevant to each story read.

12. The student will recognize the setting of a story.

Classroom Activities

8. As the conflict between the main character and another force evolves, have students make predictions about the decision the main character will make to handle the conflict. Write their predictions on the overhead or chalkboard. Then, tell students to raise their hands when one of the predictions comes true.

9. Let students watch a tape of a short popular TV show. Stop the tape midway so students can identify the main characters and conflicts. Have students predict the show's ending or resolution and clues that led them to their conclusions. Then, watch the end of the show to see the resolution of the conflict.

10. Read a relatively short, but exciting story with at least one clear conflict. Then, review the elements of a plot line, including exposition (characters and setting), rising action (conflict), climax, and resolution (ending). Give student pairs a plot line for the story and have them insert events in the appropriate place.

11. Before reading, give each student a word to listen for. As you read the passage containing the word, the student must speculate on its meaning and then verify it by checking in a dictionary.

12. Provide each student with a two-column reference card including examples of time and place words. Students can refer to the card as they conclude the setting of a story.

Time	Place
autumn	a dark street
spring	Philadelphia, PA
afternoon	on undiscovered planet
4 p.m.	Highway 51
1867	Sunset Park
dinnertime	in the attic
early one day	Edison Junior High
during senior year	Grandma's kitchen

Copyright © 1998 LinguiSystems, Inc.

Plot, Setting, Conflict, *continued*

Individual Objectives	**Classroom Activities**
13. The student will understand how setting affects the plot.	13. After reading a story, assign student pairs to change the plot based on a change in setting. For example, give one pair a time change, another a locale or cultural change, and another an environmental change. Make the changes extreme so students can compare and see the impact of setting on a story's plot.
14. The student will tell how a chapter fits into the overall scheme of a novel.	14. Teach students to review the list of chapters and titles at the beginning of the book to help them predict the plot of the novel. Make students aware that authors often use descriptive chapter titles that reflect the content of the chapter. After students read each chapter, have them think of a new title and compare it with the original title.
15. The student will follow the plot line of a novel.	15. Have students write a summary of each chapter or draw an illustration to explain its content as they read. Summaries or illustrations should focus on any conflicts and complications between characters. Then, on a mural-sized copy of a plot line, have the class add relevant information about the plot.

Literary Techniques ....

1. The student will understand the mood of a story.	1. Brainstorm words that suggest someone is sad, like *teary, miserable*, and *gloomy*. Then, play sad music while students silently read a sad story and underline sad words or sad events. Discuss the tragic mood of the story and the importance of word choices.
2. The student will recognize imagery in a story.	2. Have your students close their eyes as you read a descriptive passage aloud. Then, make a five-column chart labeled *See, Hear, Taste, Touch,* and *Smell*. In each column, list details students offer that fit each sense. Later, repeat the exercise with other stories.

Literary Techniques, *continued*

Individual Objectives

3. The student will recognize details that create suspense in a story.

4. The student will identify clues foreshadowing story events.

5. The student will understand the concept of irony.

6. The student will recognize dramatic or situational irony.

Classroom Activities

3. Provide students with the following graphic organizer to collect suspense clues. As students notice something suspenseful, they add the detail to the circle.

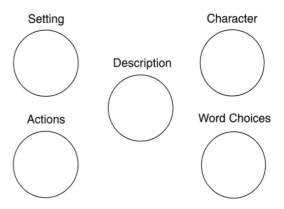

Suspense Clues

4. Read a mystery or adventure story with your students. Prepare a worksheet ahead of time listing major events from the story. In random order in the other column, list clues from the story that hinted at the events. After reading, have students match the clues with the correct event. Clues should relate to a variety of story elements, like character, dialogue, conflict, and setting.

5. Create an *Opposite of What You Expected* exercise with examples of irony from everyday situations and stories previously read. Have students match a statement of expectation with what really happened. For example, having a teacher postpone a quiz after a student actually studied would be an ironic situation.

6. Make up and role-play a story with four characters. Have four students act out part of the story. Then, send two students or "characters" out of the room, while the other two students continue the story. When the students return, ask the "audience" what they know that the two students don't as an example of dramatic irony.

Individual Objectives	**Classroom Activities**

Individual Objectives

7. The student will understand verbal irony in everyday life.

8. The student will understand verbal irony in literature.

9. The student will understand the theme of a novel or story.

10. The student will learn the types of point of view.

Classroom Activities

7. Role-play with students examples of everyday verbal irony. Have students observe body language and tone of voice as additional cues to verbal irony. For example, if a student replied to an invitation to go out for lunch with "I wouldn't want to miss lunch in the cafeteria," that student is using verbal irony.

8. Choose a story with several examples of verbal irony that prepare the reader for a twist in the plot at the end of the story. The characters Montressor and Fortunato in Edgar Allan Poe's "*Cask of the Amontillado*," for example, carry on extensive dialogue filled with verbal irony. Highlight such passages for students to interpret as they read.

9. Before reading, make a prereading questionnaire in which you ask students to rate statements related to the theme. For example, a story about wilderness survival like *My Side of the Mountain* could be preceded by statements that students rate in degrees between *Strongly Agree* to *Strongly Disagree*. See the example below.

	Strongly Agree	*Strongly Disagree*
1. I enjoy nature.	_____	_____
2. Animals should be hunted.	_____	_____
3. Anyone can survive in the wilderness.	_____	_____

10. Have students make a visual study guide to learn the points of view: personal, third person omniscient, and third person objective. For example, the omniscient point of view (all knowing, all seeing) could be represented by someone with big eyes and larger than life watching something happen between a child and his pet.

Individual Objectives

Classroom Activities

11. The student will identify the point of view of a story.

11. Make up short passages about the same event to illustrate the three points of view. For example, the personal point of view would include dialogue using *I* and the inner feelings of the main character. Third person omniscient would include dialogue and the inner feelings and thoughts from all the characters. Have students use highlight markers to locate the words that suggest the point of view. Then, have students apply the same strategy to a longer story.

12. The student will interpret symbolism in a story.

12. Have students brainstorm a list of things important in their lives. The lists should include their values, their interests and hobbies, and significant people. Then, have students make mobiles or collages using magazine pictures or their own drawings to symbolize their ideas. Follow with a discussion of how a picture or object can represent an idea and some examples of common symbols in their culture.

Figurative Language ··

1. The student will understand common figures of speech.

1. Teach or review the difference between literal and figurative language. Then, have students make picture books or posters illustrating the actual meanings of common figures of speech. Group figures of speech based on a theme or a similar connection. For example, a book of school-related sayings might include "Hit the books, Be a bookworm, She's a brain, Brown-nose the teacher," or "It's a no-brainer."

2. The student will recognize and interpret similes and metaphors.

2. Choose expressions related to a similar subject to make the concept of comparing easier to understand. For example, food-related similes and metaphors might include "Eat like a bird, as hungry as a horse, His eyes were bigger than his stomach," and "army of ants." Then, divide the sayings into simile and metaphor lists by underlining the words that help make the comparison, like *like, as, bigger than,* and *army.*

Figurative Language, *continued*

Individual Objectives	**Classroom Activities**
3. The student will identify examples of personification.	3. Make a room poster labeled with human characteristics, like *Talks, Walks,* or *Has Feelings*. Then, have students find or draw examples of personification, like the Pillsbury Doughboy that giggles, a dog that sings to its puppy girlfriend, or a tree that has a face and comes alive.
4. The student will recognize and use idioms in writing and conversation.	4. Teach a unit on idiomatic expressions, especially those used frequently in your area and those used by students of the same age. Discuss the literal and figurative meanings of each expression. Then, have students record those they hear on an everyday basis and bring them to class for discussion.
5. The student can translate slang into standard English.	5. Study theme units of slang to enrich vocabulary. For example, students could study clothing slang, like *gear, threads, bell-bottom,* and *stove-pipes*, or basketball slang like *trés* (a three pointer), *from the charity stripe*, or *slam dunk*.

Forms of Literature

Fiction

1. The student will distinguish fantasy from reality.	1. Gather several pictures that show fantastic or realistic people, creatures, settings, or events. Use pictures from sources like cartoons or comic books, fantasy stories, and magazine or news articles. Give pairs of students several pictures to sort into fantasy or reality piles. Have students discuss their reasoning.
2. The student will learn the characteristics of fairy tales.	2. Read three fairy tales. Then, make a three-column chart labeled *Characters, Setting* and *Ending*. At first, fill in the information for each story. Then, ask the students to look at the information and generalize three things that are true for all three stories.

Forms of Literature, *continued*

Individual Objectives	**Classroom Activities**
3. The student will identify the traits of a fable.	3. Introduce fables by having students recall important life lessons they've learned through personal experiences. Then, read some fables and have students conclude what life lessons the characters illustrate.
4. The student will learn the characteristics of a tall tale.	4. After reading some tall tales, provide a photograph or illustration of a real person or animal for each student. Have students "stretch" the abilities of their character and write and illustrate a story about it. Challenge students to write the tallest tale ever!
5. The student will identify the traits of a folk tale.	5. Folktales were written in an attempt to explain things that didn't make sense in a culture's environment. After reading a folktale, teach a science-related lesson that offers a scientific explanation for the phenomena presented in the folktale.
6. The student will read stories from various cultures.	6. Read a variety of stories to learn more about your students' countries of origin. Make small booklets on each culture in which students can record what they learn. Also, coordinate reading selections with classroom units, like in social studies class.
7. The student will learn about and listen to poetry.	7. Study a variety of poetry from Raffi to Shel Silverstein to Maya Angelou. Use audiotapes frequently so students can hear the flow of the language and its vivid description based on word choices and sounds. Listen to each poem several times and have students memorize and present favorite poems.
8. The student will learn the characteristics of a play.	8. Attend a community or high school theater production or arrange to get a video of a play. Discuss why an author would write a story in this form instead of as a narrative. Then, have students take a familiar short story and rewrite it as a play with dialogue, props and stage directions.

Copyright © 1998 LinguiSystems, Inc.

Individual Objectives

Classroom Activities

9. The student will recognize the elements of a comedy.

9. Let students watch a short TV show that contains visual, physical and verbal elements of comedy. Have students make a chart to record what they observe within each category. Follow by reading a short humorous story and have students analyze it for similar elements. For example, they can notice how the author uses words to create visual images.

10. The student will recognize the elements of a tragedy.

10. Have students brainstorm lists of everyday tragedies, those within our control, like those caused by careless mistakes, as well as those which are not, like getting a fatal disease. Then, discuss how tragedies in literature are often the result of unfortunate decisions characters make, like Romeo in Shakespeare's *Romeo and Juliet*. For younger students, use a story in which a character learns from a tragic mistake.

Nonfiction ··

1. The student will recognize the author's purpose in writing.

1. Review the four purposes of writing: entertainment, information, persuasion, and narration. Make a picture bulletin board or poster to remind students of the purposes, such as using a comic book picture for entertainment or a bus timetable for information.

2. The student will learn about nonfiction writing.

2. Have an It's a Fact! contest. Students gather and review examples of factual reading materials, like news articles, car manuals, cereal box labels, and encyclopedias. Discuss why authors write nonfiction — to inform, persuade, describe, or narrate an event. Then, challenge students to identify the author's purpose for each of their examples.

Individual Objectives

Classroom Activities

3. The student will learn the characteristics of biographies and autobiographies.

3. Teach a theme unit on the importance of writing about ourselves. Create a bulletin board using excerpts from biographies and autobiographies and pictures to accompany them. Have students note techniques used in this type of writing. Then, have students write biographies and autobiographies. Publish their work as small booklets including photographs and illustrations.

4. The student will learn the purpose of essays.

4. Coordinate with regular classroom teachers in choosing essays related to a current theme of study. For example, students could read an essay about the hardships and spirit of survival during pioneer times while studying about early America.

5. The student will learn the purpose of journals.

5. Have students keep their own journals for a few weeks. Assign students different topics to write about, like personal experiences, feelings about a controversial issue, and information they've learned so they see the variety of uses for a journal. Let students read examples of famous journals, like *The Diary of Anne Frank*, or the journal about Lewis and Clark's famous expedition.

Literary Concepts
The LD Teacher's IEP Companion   96   Copyright © 1998 LinguiSystems, Inc.

Attention Skills

Head down during a classroom lecture, Bret appears to be inattentive. The teacher asks a question and suddenly Bret's hand shoots up. His answer shows an absolutely uncanny understanding of what the teacher has just explained. How does he know that? Bret is an auditory learner and he's highly intelligent, but despite these strengths he doesn't earn the payoff for his intelligence by getting good grades. Despite organizational systems like assignment notebooks and colored class folders, Bret loses assignments or forgets to do them. He often sits in an after-school detention because he just can't come prepared to class, or he was moving around needlessly and distracting others. Teachers view him as lazy, apathetic and able to do better "if he tried harder" or "if he wanted to."

Bret is likely to be one of the most frustrating students you work with. With basic skills intact and high intelligence, he should be easier to deal with. But he manifests problems in areas over which only he truly has control and his performance is as inconsistent as night and day. Students like Bret may display attention problems in the form of:

- **distractibility** — The student may daydream or be distracted by inner thoughts. Or the student may be distracted by extraneous sounds and sights within the classroom.

- **impulsivity** — The student may act without planning, seeming to be careless about details and his quality of work. He may make socially inappropriate comments, causing him problems with peers and with making friends.

- **disorganization** — The student is likely to lose books and materials, misplace assignments or simply forget to do them.

- **difficulty paying attention** — The student may find it hard to concentrate during lecture-type classes and may also talk at inappropriate times. She may also find it hard to prioritize her activities and to follow through on long-term assignments.

- **physical overactivity** — The physically-overactive student may often play with a lot of objects and generally move around too much within the classroom. He may appear aggressive and have trouble following school rules for in and out of class behavior.

- **variable class performance** — The student may appear not to learn from mistakes. Her work is inconsistent in quality even on similar tasks or within similar settings or situations.

Helping Bret and others like him requires a lot of trial and error experimentation, persistence and teacher and parent support. The goals that follow will equip you and your students with objectives and strategies to help in the areas of:

- Concentration
- Quality of Work
- Task and Assignment Completion
- Eye Contact
- Listening
- Behavior and Interaction
- Memory
- Organization

Copyright © 1998 LinguiSystems, Inc.

Attention Skills

Yearly Goal: to improve attention to classroom work, behavior, and interaction

Concentration

Individual Objectives

1. The student will understand and demonstrate on-task behavior.

2. The student will remain on task long enough to complete the assignment.

3. The student will use class time provided to work on assigned tasks.

4. The student will attempt to complete a task before asking for teacher help.

5. The student will read directions and explanations before asking for teacher help.

6. The student will work for ___ minutes before requiring teacher assistance.

Classroom Activities

1. Each teacher should clarify for the student how on-task behavior looks in his classroom. For example, in one classroom it may include some free movement and quiet talk as long as the student is working on the assigned task, while another teacher may expect students to remain in their seats and work silently.

2. Initially, give the student shorter tasks so he can be successful. As the student gains success, increase the length of the task.

3. Before a student begins work on an assignment, have the student list the steps for completing it and include a time estimate for each step. As each step is completed, the student can cross it off the list.

4. Some activities or assignments may lend themselves to effort and quality grades. For example, a student could receive a good effort grade for working the first two math problems on his own and a quality grade on those problems he solves after feedback from the teacher.

5. Make it a habit to hand the more impulsive student worksheets or activities with directions and necessary explanations already underlined or highlighted to focus his attention.

6. The student who needs to increase time on task will need concrete time limits set. Provide a timer or stopwatch for the student to monitor his own work time.

Concentration, *continued*

Individual Objectives	**Classroom Activities**
7. The student will listen to a lecture, conversation or discussion without interrupting.	7. Any technique to heighten the student's interaction, such as seating him near the teacher or asking him questions, will stretch his ability to attend more appropriately.
8. The student will keep his place while reading lists of words, lines, sentences, or paragraphs.	8. Make an index card with a reading slot large enough to accommodate the amount of reading you want the student to do. As the student reads words or lines, he moves the card down uncovering the next material.
9. The student will increase awareness of and attention to relevant information and activities in his environment.	9. Some students may need specific training in sorting relevant from irrelevant information. Cue students by saying, "We'll be working on ___ for the next ten minutes. You'll need to listen closely for ___ or watch ___ closely." Repeat the same cues as needed to keep the student on track.

Quality of Work

1. The student will improve the quality of assignments.	1. With the student, review samples of her work that you consider acceptable and work that is not. Together, come up with a short checklist of reminders like the following and refer to them to ensure quality work. • Check that all items or problems are done. • Skip every other line when writing. • Write complete sentences.
2. The student will turn in assignments to the teacher for checking and for feedback on corrections.	2. Have the student staple a small slip of colored paper to the assignment to signal it's ready for review. The teacher uses the slip for comments which the student can then use as feedback to improve her performance on the task.
3. The student will have a peer or assistant check her assignments.	3. Encourage the peer or assistant to read the student's answers aloud to her as a means of checking. When the assignment has been reviewed for quality, allow the student to use a stamper with a positive message on it to indicate she has completed that step.

Copyright © 1998 LinguiSystems, Inc.

Individual Objectives	**Classroom Activities**
4. The student will complete written tasks legibly.	4. Give the student extra time to recopy an assignment so it is legible, or let the student word process assignments on computer to ensure legibility.
5. The student will turn in written assignments on clean, tear-free paper.	5. Have students keep assignments in individual notebooks so paper is handled infrequently and never torn out. For example, when a math assignment is due, the student turns in her math notebook.
6. The student will perform assignments at her academic level of ability.	6. Students need to know in which academic areas they function at or above grade level and those in which they function much lower. Sharing cumulative folder information and discussing grade history can help students understand what can reasonably be expected of them in each class and where they'll need assistance.
7. The student will perform assignments at her functional ability level.	7. Classroom assignments may need to be adjusted to fit the functional ability of the student. For example, the student may be able to multiply one-digit numbers while other students can multiply one- and two-digit numbers. Circling or otherwise indicating problems within the student's functional level clarifies what the student needs to do.

Task and Assignment Completion

1. The student will use complete phrases when writing.	1. Try to design assignments and tests or quizzes that elicit lengthier explanations or opinions so a student has to answer with phrases or sentences.
2. The student will write complete answers in sentence form.	2. Have students check for the completeness of their answers. In each question, they should underline words indicating the information being called for. Then, their answers should include a subject that relates back to the question, and a verb plus additional words that clearly explain the students' thinking.

Individual Objectives	**Classroom Activities**
3. The student will write complete sentences when reminded.	3. Each of a student's teachers should clarify his expectations for writing complete sentence answers. If this is a goal for a student, consistent expectations from teachers will help the student accomplish it.
4. The student will write complete sentences independently.	4. Make sure that any student handing in phrases as answers understands what a sentence is. Accept the assignment only after the student has written complete sentences.
5. The student will begin assignments with assistance after listening to complete directions.	5. Pair the student with an assignment buddy. This buddy can help cue the student in to when to begin and what's expected on the assignment.
6. The student will begin assignments independently after listening to complete directions.	6. A consistent auditory signal from the teacher such as "You may begin now" when instructions are completed helps a student know when to start work. Students can also be cued to ask "May I begin now?" to clarify their understanding of the appropriate beginning time.
7. The student will attempt to complete ____ out of ____ tasks assigned each class day.	7. Number and write each task expected for the day on separate colored index cards. As the student completes the task, he can hand you the appropriate card. Before assigning tasks, set the acceptable level for the day, such as six out of eight cards must be completed.
8. The student will complete all tasks assigned each class day.	8. Develop a monitoring sheet where the student records each task and the teacher signs it when each task is complete.
9. The student will record assignments correctly in an assignment notebook or organizer.	9. Teach students shorthand abbreviations for recording assignments. After a student records assignments, have his teachers sign the notebook acknowledging the accuracy of what the student wrote.
10. The student will take homework assignments home ____ out of ____ times.	10. Arrange a check-in time for students to see you before leaving for the school day. Have students bring their lists of assignments and necessary books and materials.

Attention Skills
The LD Teacher's IEP Companion

101

Copyright © 1998 LinguiSystems, Inc.

Task and Assignment Completion, *continued*

Individual Objectives

11. The student will return completed homework assignments ____ out of ____ times.

12. The student will receive help at home to complete homework assignments ____ out of ____ times.

13. The student will complete assignments and projects by the due date ____ out of ____ times.

14. The student will read assigned material ____ out of ____ times.

15. The student will study for tests or quizzes ____ out of ____ times.

16. The student will check over test or quiz answers before turning them in ____ out of ____ times.

17. The student will study and pass tests or quizzes with ____ accuracy.

Classroom Activities

11. Develop a simple check sheet to record assignment completion. Give each assignment a number and check it off when the assignment is returned.

12. Have the student's parent set aside a definite time and place to study each night. After the student is finished, have a parent initial each assignment.

13. Use a grading system that incorporates meeting timelines as well as quality. Limit the time a student has to turn in an assignment before it's half-credit or no credit. Encourage other teachers to use a similar, consistent grading system.

14. Help the student "chunk" assigned reading and spread it over a couple of sessions. Provide for review of the material and rewards for sticking with the task.

15. Graph the student's performance on tests and quizzes prior to studying as a baseline for comparison. Then, each time the student studies, record the performance on the graph and compare the increase in success.

16. Arrange for tests or quizzes to be scanned on computer so a student can use a text to speech program to read it to him. Wearing earphones and operating at his own pace allows the student to have maximum concentration.

17. To guide students' studying, set performance goals ahead of time. For example, if a student wants 70% or a C on a test, decide how much of the material he must study and know to reach the goal.

Eye Contact

1. The student will maintain eye contact with the teacher for ____ minutes at a time.

1. Stand close to the student. Signal when you want her attention and estimate a length of time, like one minute. Tell her you'll signal when it's appropriate to turn away to another task.

Copyright © 1998 LinguiSystems, Inc.

Eye Contact, *continued*

Individual Objectives

2. The student will maintain eye contact when information is being given.

3. The student will maintain eye contact when other students are speaking.

Listening

1. The student will listen quietly when other students are speaking.

2. The student will listen quietly when verbal directions are given.

3. The student will follow one-step verbal directions.

4. The student will follow two-step verbal instructions.

5. The student will follow multiple-step verbal instructions.

6. The student will independently follow two- or more-step directions.

Classroom Activities

2. Teach the student to manage her own behavior. Cue the student that you're about to give important information and review what she needs to do during this time, such as sit facing forward and keep her head up. Have her evaluate her attention and eye contact when you're done.

3. Allow the student to work with a small group of the same students each time. Arrange for interaction in a variety of situations, like other classes or the lunchroom.

1. Develop a visual signal between you and the student that indicates when it's his turn to talk or ask a question.

2. Before giving directions, make sure the student is facing forward and visually attentive. Then, use a signal like your hand behind your ear to indicate directions that require his auditory attention.

3. After giving a direction, have students restate the direction in their own words.

4. After finishing the first step of a task or assignment, have students turn over their papers as a signal. Then, give the second set of instructions and allow students to finish the task.

5. Tell students ahead of time how many steps are in the directions. Have students number their papers. After each step, students summarize what they understand to be the direction. For difficult tasks, let students work cooperatively.

6. Alleviating any anxiety about a task can help students focus better on their ability to successfully complete it. Reassure students that they have plenty of time, that they have the skills to do the task and that they will enjoy it. Share any past successful experiences by other students.

Copyright © 1998 LinguiSystems, Inc.

Individual Objectives

7. The students will follow verbal directions in the correct sequence.

8. The student will follow verbal directions and complete a task with _____% accuracy.

Behavior and Interaction ···

1. With reminders, the student will respond appropriately to what other students say.

2. On her own, the student will respond appropriately to what other students say.

3. The student will react appropriately to stimuli in her environment, like bells or PA announcements.

4. The student will walk quietly through the halls.

Classroom Activities

7. Discuss what would happen if steps are done out of order. Encourage students to draw picture cues related to the directions to remind them of the order.

8. For practice, design a variety of exercises in which completely following the directions ensures 100% accuracy. Then, have students complete tasks on their own and record their levels of accuracy.

1. Role-play with the student two to three things she can say when interacting with another student. She may ask a question, pay a compliment or add information of her own relevant to what was said. When the student responds appropriately, provide positive feedback.

2. Arrange for the student to carry a card teachers sign each day when her interaction with other students has been appropriate. Discuss ahead of time the rewards or consequences for good behavior over a certain length of time.

3. Post visual reminders in the room and/or at the student's desk with tips for handling classroom interruptions. For example:

> PA announcements are important. During an announcement:
>
> • Make sure you're in your seat.
> • Listen carefully.
> • Ask the teacher to explain, if necessary.

4. Demonstrate for the student what's expected as she travels through the halls. As she goes to music class, show her the most direct route and how to move down the right side of the hallway quietly and without touching things. Practice each situation before the student moves independently.

Individual Objectives	**Classroom Activities**
5. The student will move quietly with a group.	5. To ensure success, pair the student with a buddy who's able to move quietly through the hallway.
6. The student will work quietly in places like the library or computer center.	6. Supervise initial visits and role-play appropriate behavior with the student. Then, arrange with the librarian or computer assistant to sign a Privilege Pass the student carries with her acknowledging her appropriate behavior.
7. The student will care for school materials properly.	7. Allow students to pass out materials frequently after reminders about how to handle them. Remove materials from any student misusing them.
8. The student will interact with other students appropriately in the lunchroom, at recess, or during class free time.	8. Make it a habit to eat lunch with your students once a week. Model appropriate lunchroom behavior for them, such as waiting patiently in line, thanking the servers, taking your seat, and cleaning up when done. Students will love the one-on-one attention, too.
9. The student will wait her turn in activities and games.	9. Initially, put a student with only one other student to take turns. As the student's ability to wait increases, increase the number of students involved in the activity.
10. The student will display appropriate interaction skills in supervised structured activities or games.	10. Review game rules and expected behavior before students engage in any activities or games.
11. The student will display appropriate interaction skills in minimally supervised, structured activities or games.	11. For many students, a physical education class may be a minimally supervised structured time if there's a choice of activities. Before a student goes to gym class, discuss what activity she may choose. Talk about the behavior expected during the activity, like taking turns or putting equipment away.
12. The student will demonstrate appropriate interaction skills in unstructured situations, like lunchtime or recess.	12. Allow the student to choose with whom and where she sits or plays, as long as the interaction is appropriate. Regularly throughout the week, monitor her progress and provide feedback.

Copyright © 1998 LinguiSystems, Inc.

Individual Objectives	**Classroom Activities**
13. The student will ask permission to use another's materials or possessions.	13. Whether at home or school, students should ask to use items that are not theirs. Communicate your expectations about borrowing behavior to the students' parents. Encourage parents to follow through with similar rules and expectations at home.
14. The student will seek attention by standing quietly or raising her hand.	14. Reinforce your classroom rules frequently. Before a quiet activity, remind students to raise their hands if they need help or to quietly walk to you for assistance. Ignore students who don't follow the rules.
15. The student will learn to raise her hand before answering.	15. Recognize the student only when her hand is raised. If the student blurts out an answer, ignore it and recognize a student who has raised his hand as a way of modeling appropriate behavior for the other student.
16. The student will only make comments relevant to the current situation.	16. Keeping students focused on the topic of the discussion can eliminate irrelevant comments. Saying "Who has something to say about _____?" or "Does anyone have questions about _____?" reminds students of appropriate things to talk about.
17. The student will not say inappropriate things or make inappropriate sounds in the classroom.	17. Provide an alternative outlet for the student's impulsive comments or sounds. If the student can write, have her put her thoughts and comments in a notebook when tempted to act inappropriately. Later, you can discuss the nature of the comments and praise the student for her self-control.
18. The student will wait for her turn to talk in interactions with peers.	18. To increase success, provide many opportunities for small group interaction so students interact frequently. As the student becomes more skillful at listening to others and responding appropriately, increase the size of the group.
19. The student will say what she has to say within an appropriate length of time.	19. With the student, develop a signal to use when she talks beyond a reasonable time limit. For example, simply raising your index finger could be a subtle signal to the student.

Individual Objectives	Classroom Activities
20. The student will sit appropriately in her seat.	20. If possible, place the student in a desk and chair that won't tip. Or seat the student in a study carrel to prevent distractions that cause the student to move about needlessly.
21. The student will move around the classroom only as needed.	21. Provide appropriate reasons for the student to leave her seat. For example, the student can get her materials from a shelf or run an errand for the teacher.
22. The student will keep hands to herself when others are nearby.	22. Seating a student in inner rows eliminates the number of students who pass by during activities such as using the pencil sharpener or turning in papers. Seating a student near the teacher or an aide also helps monitor the behavior.
23. The student will not make noises with objects.	23. Students should always have other, easier work to turn to when they're finished so they don't distract others. Eliminate unnecessary objects from the student's desk, too.
24. The student will recognize when she is restless and needs a physical break from an activity.	24. Work out a signal with the student that indicates she is having trouble focusing. Provide a special place in the classroom where the student can go. Have hands-on activities like clay or objects to put together for the student to work out her feelings. Agree on a length of time beforehand for such a break.
25. The student will try to control her nervous activity, like tapping pencils or biting nails.	25. To help the student stay focused on the activity, move about the room and interact frequently with her.
26. The student will use self-control when feeling angry, frustrated or otherwise upset.	26. Teach the student steps of problem solving. Encourage the student to first recognize her feelings, the possible problem and what she can do about it. Stress the need to think of how others will react if the student makes a certain decision.
27. The student will solve conflicts with peers.	27. Build in a class time to demonstrate and apply conflict management. Using generic characters and typical classroom situations, have students role-play solutions while also enhancing communication skills.

Attention Skills
The LD Teacher's IEP Companion   107   Copyright © 1998 LinguiSystems, Inc.

Behavior and Interaction, *continued*

Individual Objectives	**Classroom Activities**

Individual Objectives

28. The student will make appropriate physical contact, like respecting physical space or shaking hands.

29. The student will follow the rules for group games or activities.

30. The student will smoothly change from one activity to another.

31. The student will change behavior to fit the situation.

32. The student will calm down within _____ minutes of recess or another activity.

33. The student will monitor her own work time.

34. The student will remain on task despite visual or auditory stimuli in the classroom.

35. The student will remove herself from an activity when self-control is threatened.

Classroom Activities

28. Provide new experiences for students to learn appropriate behaviors. For example, challenge another class to a kickball game. Greet each other with handshakes. Later, congratulate the winners with "high-fives."

29. Write out a simplified explanation of rules for the activity or game or review them verbally ahead of time. Then, select a small group with which the student can interact.

30. Give students ample warning when an activity will change. For example, announcing "You have five minutes of work time left before we . . ." or flipping the light switch on and off will help students prepare for the transition.

31. Give the student a schedule of the day's activities so she can prepare for what comes next. Allow transition time between activities.

32. Provide the student with a quieter place like a study carrel or a quiet study area to help her make the adjustment to a new situation before joining the rest of the class.

33. Set clear time limits for assignments or activities. Write the time on the chalkboard or a slip of paper on the student's desk. Provide a timer for the student to monitor her own work time.

34. Teach the student how to handle outside stimuli. If there's too much auditory stimuli, the student can ask to move to another seat. Sitting in a study carrel can help the student control visual stimuli.

35. Teach students to say "I need a time out" and arrange a chair or cushion in a quiet corner where the student can regain control. Make sure the student's other teachers make similar arrangements.

Behavior and Interaction, *continued*

Individual Objectives

36. The student will use a voice level appropriate to the situation.

Classroom Activities

36. Demonstrate what different voice levels sound like and when it's appropriate to use them. Draw a "noise indicator" on the chalkboard to signal which voice to use for a given situation or activity. When voice levels are too high, point to where they should be on the noise indicator. Individual students needing help with voice control can have pictures of indicators at their desks for the teacher to point to as she moves about the room.

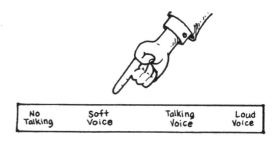

Memory

1. The student will remember materials for a task or assignment.

1. Create a materials list for each class. Prior to class, help the student circle materials that will be needed that day. The student then gathers and brings the necessary items.

2. The student will memorize short amounts of information for class, like a poem or a formula.

2. Let students practice memorizing by recording on tape. First, they can record while looking at the material and then listening to themselves. Eventually let students work up to recording the information from memory.

3. The student will remember information after a short period of time.

3. Let students put small chunks of information, like new social studies terms, on flash cards. The word can be on the front and its definition on the back. Have students choose a few terms to study at a time. Within five minutes, show students the terms and ask for definitions. Review the material again during the class period and at the end. Set minimum goals of what the student should know within a given period of time, such as five of ten new social studies terms within the hour.

Copyright © 1998 LinguiSystems, Inc.

Individual Objectives

4. The student will remember information after a long interval, such as several hours.

5. The student will remember the daily routine, like going to lunch or lining up for dismissal.

Classroom Activities

4. For things like test preparation or initial concept teaching, arrange for the student to review the material twice in one day. You or another teacher or peer tutor can reinforce the earlier teaching and review. Set minimum standards for what the student should know within the time period.

5. Make a small flip chart, with one page at a time reviewing the daily routine. As the day unfolds, flip over the chart and review as you begin that part of the day.

Organization

1. The student will have materials needed for an assigned task.

1. Give the student a written list of materials before a task. Direct the student as to the appropriate time to gather these materials and have them ready. Color code the lists for each class, like pink for math or yellow for science. Information on each list might include:

   Math Class

   _____ math workbook
   _____ pencil
   _____ paper
   _____ calculator
   _____ yesterday's homework

2. The student will carry materials in an appropriate way to ensure getting them to class.

2. Meet with students during registration or orientation to discuss things like book bags and individual class folders. Then, review students' schedules and write out plans for what to carry and when so students come to class prepared and on time.

Copyright © 1998 LinguiSystems, Inc.

Organization, *continued*

Individual Objectives	Classroom Activities
3. The student will organize his locker or desk to facilitate locating materials and assignments.	3. Hold weekly locker or desk checks. Reward students for good organization.
4. The student will put completed work in a designated place.	4. In your class or other teachers' classes, make sure students understand when and where to turn in completed assignments. Since directions may vary, students may require a list reminding them to put their assignments in the green box in Mrs. Lyle's room or in their individual folder in Ms. Garcia's room.
5. The student will have materials ready and be prepared to work at the start of class.	5. Because bells and other signals are often hard to hear in the hustle and bustle of students coming into a classroom, a visual signal may be more effective. Hold up a green card labeled "Ready to Begin" to signal the start of class.
6. The student will do the steps of an assigned task in sequential order.	6. With the student, summarize and make a short checklist of steps to complete for a task. Have the student check off the steps as he finishes.
7. The student will prioritize and complete assignments with teacher help.	7. Set up a regular daily meeting to look at the student's assignment book. Have the student number assignments in the order they should be done.
8. The student will prioritize and complete assignments independently.	8. Students need to know different systems for prioritizing or organizing. Assignments can be prioritized by the amount of time needed and materials needed (especially if they're long term), by time of day of a class, or by level of difficulty. Encourage students to plan based on their needs and strengths.

Copyright © 1998 LinguiSystems, Inc.

Study and Organizational Skills

"Where's your assignment, Mike?" I ask. "I think it's in my locker," Mike replies. So I send Mike off to his locker wishfully thinking just this once he'll return with assignment in hand.

How many times have you had the same conversation with your "Mikes"? Mike's answer could mean many things:

- My assignment is done, but I'm clueless as to its whereabouts.

- I have no idea what you're talking about because I didn't even know I had an assignment.

- I didn't understand the assignment so I didn't do it.

- I didn't write the assignment down or take my books home.

Whatever the reason, students like Mike complicate their situations by layering poor study and organizational skills on top of their learning disabilities. Developing good study and organizational habits, like using an assignment notebook, taking notes, and seeking extra help ensure success for most of our students within the regular classroom.

The objectives and activities that follow will help your students develop better study and organizational skills by acquiring strategies for:

- Organizes and Locating Information
- Reads Textbooks Effectively
- Completes Assignments
- Takes Notes from Classroom Lessons
- Takes Notes from Written Material
- Studies for and Takes Tests

Study and Organizational Skills

Yearly Goal: to learn and apply study skills for successful class performance

Organizes and Locates Information ....

Individual Objectives

1. The student will recognize and use alphabetical order.

2. The student will find words in a picture dictionary.

3. The student will locate words in a glossary.

4. The student will locate words in a dictionary.

5. The student will choose appropriate meanings in a dictionary or glossary.

Classroom Activities

1. Discuss all the possible ways reading information could be organized. Entertain even the zaniest of ideas, such as organizing information by the length of a word or putting words together that sound alike. Then, refer to the alphabet as a common reference point for organizing much of our information. Bring in samples of materials organized alphabetically, like phone books and encyclopedias.

2. Make and tape horizontal alphabet strips to students' desks. Then, have students do word searches. Let them look up a favorite animal. Then, have them look up animals whose letters come before and after their favorite animal.

3. As students read from a passage, have them write down any words that seem to be emphasized, either by repeated use or bold-faced type. Later, have students look up the words in the glossary. Compare and contrast the uses of a glossary and a dictionary.

4. Create a Can You Find It? game. Type individual words and two blanks on card-sized paper. Have students work in pairs to locate the page where a word would be found. Then, have students write the guide words on the two blanks.

5. Because dictionaries or glossaries offer multiple word meanings, students should first predict and write down what the word might mean. Then, they can check their prediction with the closest meaning.

Organizes and Locates Information, *continued*

Organizes and Locates Information, *continued*

Individual Objectives	Classroom Activities
6. The student will use a table of contents to locate information.	6. Initially, give students broad categories of information usually covered in a table of contents. For example, students might look up insects in their science books. Encourage students to scan the table of contents of any book to become familiar with its overall contents. Then, give students more specific information to research, like the arthropods, a subgroup of insects, so they learn how to fine tune their searches.
7. The student will use an index.	7. Have students make a chart comparing and contrasting a dictionary with an index. Under the *Alike* column, students might write "arranged alphabetically," while under the *Different* column, students might indicate that an index includes more information. Give students sample situations and ask them if they'd use a dictionary or an index. For example, a dictionary would give a basic definition of democracy while an index would lead to more extensive information about The Declaration of Independence.
8. The student will look for a topic by using subentries.	8. Before students research a topic, have them brainstorm related topics they may find information under. Students can complete a word web with the initial word in the middle and related words on lines outside the word. When students locate a word in the index, they should write the page number referred to on the same line for future reference.
9. The student will locate appropriate resources for a given project or assignment.	9. Design a planning sheet for students to use prior to beginning a project. On the sheet, students state the purpose of their project as well as likely resources for their information, like an atlas, almanac, encyclopedia, the Internet, or personal interviews. Students submit the planning sheet for review prior to being allowed access to a library or computer lab.

Copyright © 1998 LinguiSystems, Inc.

Individual Objectives

Classroom Activities

10. The student will use the Internet to search for current resources.

10. Many schools require Internet training before a student may use it. Have students complete such training as part of an English or social studies class, for example. Then, have students research topics on the Internet prior to beginning new units. For example, students might research about Langston Hughes, Malcom X or Martin Luther King before a unit on Civil Rights.

Reads Textbooks Effectively ···

1. The student can locate words an author feels is important.

1. Get an extra copy of a content area book that can be marked up. Then, go through a chapter the student is currently studying allowing the student to use a highlight pen to highlight bold and italicized words as well as the definitions or relevant information helping to identify them.

2. The student recognizes the purpose of headings and subheadings.

2. Prepare a study guide for a chapter organized in outline form using the headings and subheadings. Read the outline and discuss what students are about to learn. Then, read the chapter together and have students add details to the outline. After much practice, have students create their own outline study guides for chapters.

3. The student reads and interprets captions to pictures and illustrations.

3. Have students preview a chapter by reading side material, like charts, diagrams, pictures, and captions. Then, as they read the chapter, they'll understand the connection of the side material to concepts covered in the chapter.

4. The student will follow a diagram, chart or time line.

4. Preteach reading diagrams, charts or time lines prior to students actually encountering the information in reading. For example, make a time line of recent community events students can relate to prior to reading about a time line of events about the Civil War in their history books.

Copyright © 1998 LinguiSystems, Inc.

Individual Objectives

5. The student can read a map to answer questions.

6. The student will find information using bar, line, pie, and pictographs.

7. The student will apply the SQ3R reading technique.

Completes Assignments

1. The student can plan assignments within a time frame.

2. The student will list and prioritize assignments to be completed.

Classroom Activities

5. Enlarge maps with details that are hard to read. Add any color coding or color outlining to help make it easier for students to locate information.

6. While preparing an instructional unit about graphs, use a theme to hold concepts together for students. Also, use a variety of graphs to present the same information so students can gain and relate the skills of interpretation. For example, a theme unit on Eating Out could incorporate bar, line, pie, and pictographs picturing customers' most frequent meal choices.

7. Let students preview reading material as partners. Have partners take turns completing each of the steps: survey, question, read, recite, and review. Let partners audiotape specific steps, like the recite and review steps, to be used later to review concepts.

1. With students, write out the smaller steps needed to complete an assignment. Include the due date as well as personal time the student needs to mentally process the task and then complete it. If a student needs an accommodation because of her learning disability, she needs to arrange that, also. Then, have the student check off the steps as she completes them.

2. Each student should keep an assignment notebook as part of his "contract for services" from the resource teacher. At the end of each class, the student should record the next assignment and indicate even if there isn't one. The student can then have the regular education teacher sign off on the assignment or arrange a daily check-in point with the resource teacher to get help planning and prioritizing assignments.

Completes Assignments, *continued*

Individual Objectives	Classroom Activities
3. The student will bring materials needed for class.	3. Have the student's teacher sign off in the student's assignment notebook when the student has brought the required materials. Let the student earn free time or other rewards after so many days of good preparation.
4. The student will keep her desk or locker orderly.	4. Establish a weekly locker or desk check. Reorganize stray papers into class folders. Have the student check for any incomplete or not turned in assignments.
5. The student will stay on task during work time.	5. Make sure students have a clear under-standing of how long they have to work. Set up benchmarks, like "You should have Section A done by 10:00," so students can plan accordingly.
6. The student will organize class folders or notebooks in a logical way.	6. Choose different colored folders or notebooks for each class. Stress the importance of writing assignments in the assignment notebook, of only doing math homework in the red notebook and so on.
7. The student will develop and follow a daily study schedule.	7. Coordinate an after-school study time with the student's parents. After the student has completed work, parents can sign off on a chart indicating what and how long the student studied. Encourage parents to provide rewards for getting started independently and staying on task.
8. The student will modify a daily study schedule according to assignment or schedule changes.	8. During the student's study time, encourage him to review when assignments are due and any upcoming changes in schedule that might affect them. Have the student star items that have become a priority for completion.
9. The student will check over completion and quality of work.	9. At the bottom of each assignment, require the student to sign off that he has followed all steps of the assignment and completed it to the best of his ability.

I've done every math problem and shown my work. I've checked it over to the best of my ability.

Josh Mersman

Completes Assignments, *continued*

Individual Objectives	Classroom Activities
10. The student will recognize when help is needed.	10. Provide students with alternatives when they find schoolwork frustrating. Rather than crumpling up an assignment, have the student use a signal, such as turning his paper over to signal a need for more explanation or help.
11. The student will break long-term assignments into several smaller ones.	11. Using index cards, have students write down each smaller step required to complete a larger assignment. As the student completes a step, she can cross it off or throw away the card.
12. The student will use an appropriate place to study.	12. Have parents set up a special study area at home with minimal distractions. Provide study carrels stocked with school supplies for students to study in while at school.
13. The student will turn in assignments to the correct person at the designated time.	13. For every assignment, encourage students to immediately write the following information in an agreed upon place on notebook paper.

Name:
Class:
Assignment Description:
Date due:
Hand in completed assignment to:

Students can then arrange assignment papers in a three-ring binder according to class and then according to time due within the class section.

14. The student will monitor completion of daily assignments.	14. Develop a grade-tracking sheet for each class that includes date and description of each assignment, and grade/points received. Also, include a spot for test and quiz results. As each assignment or test is completed, students fill in the information. Students can periodically evaluate what percent of class work they've completed, and the quality of that work.

Study and Organizational Skills
The LD Teacher's IEP Companion

Copyright © 1998 LinguiSystems, Inc.

Takes Notes from Classroom Lessons ··

Individual Objectives

1. The student will write words dictated by the teacher.

2. The student will write simple sentences dictated by the teacher.

3. The student will write notes from a class presentation when the teacher directs.

4. The student will copy notes from the board or overhead projector.

5. The student will identify key words by how they're written in board notes or in listening guides.

6. The student will listen for vocal emphasis and syntactical clues to identify key words and ideas.

7. The student will write notes using a few key words to condense important information.

Classroom Activities

1. Audiotape individual words for students to listen to. Make sure the words are within the students' spelling vocabulary. Allow students to start and stop the tape as needed, eventually working up to keeping pace with the speed of the dictation.

2. As part of a lesson review, write sentences as a class summarizing main points learned. Then, dictate the sentences for the students to record.

3. As a matter of routine, students should have an open notebook on their desks to record information as the teacher directs. Use key words, such as "It's important to remember" or "The three causes of the war were . . ." to cue students when to take notes.

4. Remind students to take down information the way the teacher wrote it. The format of the notes as well as the content can be important for future tests or quizzes. Encourage students to check their notes against the teacher's for any missing words or misspellings.

5. Develop consistent visual methods to help students recognize important information. For example, bold face important words in a listening guide or use colored chalk to underline key words on the chalkboard.

6. Create a mock lecture on audiotape. As students detect vocal emphasis or syntactical clues, they should take notes. Later, they can check their notes against yours.

7. Review the concepts of recognizing main idea and new vocabulary. Then, using short "lecture type" passages on audiotape, have students summarize main ideas and list any new words from what they hear.

Individual Objectives

8. The student will organize notes using outline form.

9. The student will take notes using semantic webbing.

Classroom Activities

8. Prepare partially filled in outlines for students to complete as they listen to a class lesson. Eventually have students create their own outlines and compare them with your model.

9. Model semantic webbing as a lead-in to a lesson. Assess students' prior knowledge of a topic and fill in categories on a web. As the lesson continues, have students add information to appropriate topics on the web.

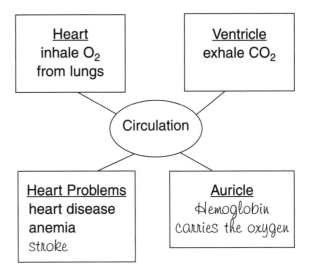

10. The student will diagram notes about a sequence of events using boxes and arrows.

10. To practice sequencing, make a worksheet with boxes and arrows. Fill in the boxes with information that must be sequenced or that shows a cause and effect relationship. Arrange the boxes in random order on the worksheet. Then, have students cut out the boxes and arrows and put them in the correct order. Later, prepare a graphic organizer students can use any time you present notes requiring a sequence or diagram.

Copyright © 1998 LinguiSystems, Inc.

Takes Notes from Written Material ••

Individual Objectives

1. The student can copy written information word for word.

2. The student will use print features, like bold print and italics, to recognize important information.

3. The student will recognize headings and subheadings as key information to write.

4. The student can shorten written information into a few key words.

5. The student will identify and then outline main points and supporting details.

6. The student will use boxes, lines and/or arrows to write notes and show relationships or the sequence of information.

Classroom Activities

1. Practice with small amounts initially, working on adding more lines as copying becomes more accurate. Have students hold an index card under the spot where they're copying so they don't lose necessary material.

2. Make worksheet exercises using sample text from science and social studies textbooks. Then, have students use a highlight marker to mark off the information surrounding the bold or italicized word that is important to know. Students often will use just the information after the word. Have students read the entire sentence aloud that surrounds the word so they recognize all the important information.

3. After reading each section of a chapter separated by the heading or subheading, have students write the heading or subheading. Then, have them write a brief summary of the main idea in that section.

4. Conduct several lessons in paraphrasing, moving from short amounts of information to longer passages. Then, give students a passage for practice. Highlight areas of importance, if needed.

5. Teach students a variety of organizational techniques for recording notes. They can use techniques, like section or chapter questions, the organization of the reading, or *who-what-where-when-why-how* questions.

6. Prepare study guides using boxes, lines and arrows for sections of a prior unit as a model. Discuss why the material was presented visually in this manner. Use other organizing techniques for the rest of the unit. Then, have small groups prepare their own study guides for the next chapter. Encourage the use of a computer to record their ideas so the material will be easier to reproduce for all group members.

Studies for and Takes Tests

Individual Objectives

1. The student will determine information relevant to the test.

2. The student will plan time for test study.

3. The student will learn content-area vocabulary.

4. The student will practice answering a variety of question formats.

5. The student will read test directions and ask for clarification as needed.

Classroom Activities

1. Students can develop a form to fill out each time a test is announced. The student can fill out the form independently or stay after class for teacher help. The form should request information like:

   - date
   - material to be covered, notes or other material included
   - types of questions
   - point value of test

2. Provide the student with a blank weekly or monthly calendar showing the days before the test. With the student, designate specific study times and the activity to use, like reviewing notes, rereading the chapter or reviewing orally with the teacher.

3. Tests often cover content-area vocabulary extensively. To review, students can make vocabulary flash cards with the term on the front and its meaning on the back. Let students quiz each other or create games like Jeopardy using terms.

4. Get samples of previous tests given for a class so students can practice with a variety of formats. Have students read through directions and project time needed to complete the test. Then, go over test items with students and share relevant test-taking tips.

5. Train students in a direction-reading process. With a colored highlighter, have students highlight key words in written directions and read through each set. Have them notice how test items change in each section. Encourage students to ask for clarification of any directions.

Individual Objectives	Classroom Activities
6. The student will make sample tests or study guides to study for tests.	6. Students can study and improve test-taking skill by creating tests for current content studied. By looking at vocabulary, chapter questions and key ideas, students should predict test questions and make sample tests with a variety of question formats. Students can exchange and take each others' tests as a way of studying.
7. The student will ask for any needed test accommodations.	7. Prior to a test, students should meet with their regular education teacher to discuss the kind of test questions that will be included. At that time, they should request any modifications needed, such as a time extension or recording answers on an audiotape.
8. The student will interpret directions and plan answers for short essays.	8. Have students practice planning answers for short essays that ask them to explain, to compare and contrast, to list, to justify, and so on. Give students topics relevant to current content studied. Then, have them create a chart to plan out a comparison and contrast answer or to list the pros or cons for a justification answer. Give feedback on their planning.
9. The student will learn to write short essay answers.	9. Students can develop a tip sheet to check that short answers are complete. The sheet might include tips like: • Did I do what the question asked — explained, listed, justified, described, etc.? • Have I answered all parts of the question? • Have I checked my spelling and grammar?
10. The student will learn a strategy for multiple-choice type tests.	10. Have the students read the questions and then formulate their own answers. If needed for each question, have the student write his answers on a separate sheet of paper. Then, tell the student to choose the multiple-choice answer that most resembles his answer.
11. The student will learn a strategy for true-false statements.	11. Remind students to read the statement thoroughly a couple of times. For a statement to be true, every part of it must be true.

Classroom Behavior

Envision this scenario: the same class, same teacher, different students, both with learning disabilities. James strolls in tardy, often without a book, paper or pencil. In a group activity, he fades and lets others carry the load. Assignments are often incomplete or never turned in. Though very intelligent and capable of handling the regular class curriculum, he is failing. His resource teacher has arranged accommodations for James, but he's inconsistent in requesting or using them.

Amanda's assignments are always turned in. Tardiness is never a problem; she's frequently early checking in with the teacher on the plan for the day. As a participant in a group activity, she makes it quite clear that she has a learning disability. She also makes it perfectly clear that she intends to carry her load and she expects others to do so, also. Amanda, too, is highly intelligent, but she has more severe reading and writing disabilities than James. Even so, she is thriving in the regular education environment and she knows when and what kind of help to get from her resource teacher.

Why is there such a discrepancy in the performance of two students who obviously have the skills and intelligence to succeed in a regular education classroom? Amanda has learned appropriate classroom behavior. She knows what "normal" classroom behavior looks like and she uses it to her advantage. She calls attention to her disability only when she needs to, otherwise blending in as a "regular kid" who demands no more work of the teacher than any other student in the classroom.

The objectives and activities that follow will help your students develop the classroom behaviors of:

- Follows Directions
- Interacts in Groups
- Works Independently
- Accepts Responsibility for Behavior

Classroom Behavior

Yearly Goal: to develop the appropriate behavior for learning and interacting

Follows Directions ....

Individual Objectives

1. The student will look and listen during short conversations.

2. The student will look and listen during classroom directions and discussions.

3. The student will pay attention during the entire period of directions.

4. The student will locate written directions.

5. The student will follow oral directions the first time they're given.

Classroom Activities

1. Some students who have trouble following classroom directions have difficulty attending to small group interactions. Give these students plenty of practice in participating and listening. Set up pair sharing times as part of classroom activities. Designate one student the "talker" and the other the "listener," then have students reverse roles. Verbally reward for looking at and listening to partners.

2. Stand close to a student who has trouble initiating attention. You may want to quietly say the student's name and tell him you're about to give some important information.

3. Cue students when it's time to follow directions. A simple, "It's time to look and listen for directions," may be effective. Using a consistent technique, such as putting directions on the overhead while you say them is also helpful.

4. Teach students the language of directions, like *circle, draw, underline, complete*, and so on. Have students underline the direction words and paraphrase the directions before proceeding.

5. Break your own habit of repeating directions. If you repeat directions, students see no need to listen the first time and will get in the habit of ignoring directions until several reminders have been given.

Follows Directions, *continued*

Individual Objectives	Classroom Activities
6. The student will read the entire set of directions before beginning work.	6. Have the student circle or highlight in color what she interprets to be the directions. Then, have the student read them aloud to you and discuss if the directions seem logical and complete.
7. The student follows written or oral directions at the appropriate time, like for a tornado drill or lunch time rules.	7. Discuss school rules versus classroom rules. Compare the need to follow school rules for safety, scheduling or time reasons to the need to follow classroom rules which focus more on respecting others and creating an effective learning environment.
8. The student will ask questions to clarify written or oral directions.	8. Encourage students to ask specific questions about the directions, rather than saying, "I don't get how to do this."
9. The student follows daily classroom routines, such as raise your hand before talking, or put your books away when the bell rings.	9. Students learning basic classroom routines may need structured behavioral plans. For example, a student can earn a point for each rule he follows during the day and then converts points into a reward.
10. The student takes notes about directions to follow at a later time, like homework or returning a permission form.	10. Have a daily *Things to Remember* corner on your chalkboard. Initially, check students' assignment notebooks to see that they've recorded the day's "things to remember."

Interacts in Groups

Participates in Play and Group Activities ···

1. The student will participate in play activities with other children.	1. Arrange situations for the student to become familiar with other students. For example, partners can be sent to take attendance to the office together.
2. The student listens to and follows the rules of an organized activity.	2. Before participating in the activity, have the student paraphrase her understanding of the activity and its rules.
3. The student will share books, toys or other materials with peers.	3. Allow the student to select some toys or books to share while keeping others for her own use. That way, she'll feel she has some control over her sharing.

Individual Objectives

Classroom Activities

4. The student will take turns with others in an activity or game.

4. Make sure the student understands how to take turns for a particular activity, such as moving clockwise in a group, or after a team scores so many points in a game, and so on.

5. The student will refrain from using physical force with others.

5. Collect baseline data indicating under what circumstances the student is using physical force. Then, teach the student replacement strategies for handling his aggression. For example, if he acts out because a group hasn't allowed him to join in, he can let the teacher know what group he'd like to join and the teacher can model the process for joining.

6. The student will have a level of energy appropriate to the activity.

6. As you change activities, make sure students understand the type of movement and level of talking that are acceptable. For example, during game time, louder talking is okay, time limits are more generous, and some physical movement is expected. During a group assignment, however, quiet talking and attentive listening to group members is expected.

7. The student will compromise her own wishes to meet the wishes of the group.

7. Teach the student strategies for handling the disappointment of "not getting her way." For example, the student may tell herself, "I didn't get my way this time, but I'll have another chance later."

8. The student will ask permission to use others' things.

8. Role-play the correct way to ask to use something. Encourage the entire class to use similar language in their requests.

Is a Cooperative Group Member ·

1. The student will cooperate within a group.

1. Carefully select group members ahead of time for a particular activity. Keeping group size to two or three members ensures that everyone contributes and feels a sense of belonging.

Interacts in Groups, *continued*

Individual Objectives	**Classroom Activities**

2. The student contributes to a group effort.

3. The student accepts losing in a game or activity.

4. The student will accept help from others.

5. The student will offer help to others.

6. The student understands and accepts the limitations and differences of others.

7. The student displays appropriate amount of self-control for an activity or game.

2. Structure activities and assignments with clearly defined roles so equal contribution is a given. Provide a written description of the roles and expected behavior.

3. As an incentive for good sportsmanship, allow the student to select the next activity or game, or to be first the next time.

4. Read stories about famous and everyday people who have reached goals through the help of others. Discuss the benefits of sharing responsibility and helping each other to reach common goals.

5. Create a classroom community of helpers. Rather than you the teacher always being the helper, recognize and use the strengths of students to help one another. For example, allow another student to write a story as a student with a writing disability dictates it. Stress how creative the storyteller is and how he needs a partner to capture his ideas as they speed out of his head!

6. Prepare the student prior to her encounter with a student different from herself. Explain the other student's abilities and needs. Discuss how the student may expect to feel and how she can help him.

7. Verbally rehearse with the student what he should say to himself as he participates. For example, "I need to keep my hands away from the game board until it's my turn." Adapt the verbal messages to the kind of activity.

Copyright © 1998 LinguiSystems, Inc.

Accomplishes Work as Part of a Group ···

Individual Objectives

1. The student will have appropriate listening and attention skills to participate in group work.

2. The student will complete an individual goal as part of a group plan.

3. The student uses an appropriate voice level for group work.

4. The student will make remarks relevant to the group activity.

5. The student will listen to the ideas and opinions of others.

6. The student will take turns and not interrupt others.

Classroom Activities

1. Some students may need a smaller group to work with to help them build attention and listening skills. Keeping a student with the same students for several activities can also help her build the confidence to interact appropriately.

2. Once the group has decided roles and responsibilities for group members, briefly meet with the group. Write each student's responsibilities on an index card to keep in front of him as a reminder and to check off as he completes them.

3. Students will need specific guidelines for voice levels. Explain to students to use talking voices while in groups so the noise level in the room doesn't interfere with the ability of a group to work.

4. Tell groups their task is to stay focused on the activity, both in terms of what they're doing and what they're discussing. Circulate around the room carrying a tally card on which you record points for sticking with the activity.

5. Make an audiotape of several students expressing different opinions about a topic. Have the listening student imagine she is part of the group. Pause the tape after a speaker and have the student respond to the other student's ideas. Coach her on appropriate ways to agree or disagree and how to know when it's okay to give your opinion.

6. Some students may need coaching during group discussions or group work. Cues, like "Serena, now would be a good time to tell us what you think about . . ." will help students develop the sense of timing their comments.

Interacts in Groups, *continued*

Individual Objectives

7. The student will use socially acceptable language.

8. The student will express opinions and needs in a group.

9. The student will respect group leadership.

10. The student stays on task within a group.

11. The student will accept personal responsibility for helping meet a group goal.

Classroom Activities

7. Remind students to listen to others' opinions and ideas without judging them. Remove any student from a group whose comments are negative or who uses inappropriate language.

8. Number index cards to reflect the number of group members. Then, have students choose a card whose number indicates the order in which they contribute ideas, needs or opinions to the group.

9. Make sure students understand the role of a group leader. List responsibilities on the chalkboard. Rotate leadership opportunities so all students gain experience being leaders.

10. Before a group activity, list the leader's responsibilities and the responsibilities of group members, such as:

Group Leader	Group Members
1. Lead discussion on the topic.	1. Offer ideas about the topic.
2. Summarize the group's ideas.	2. Write your ideas on paper to hand in.
3. Present the group's ideas to the class.	3. Listen while group leaders present.

Move among groups frequently praising them for on-task behavior.

11. Teach group members how to decide on "action points." Before a group concludes a meeting, have individual group members write down what they need to contribute next to the group project and when it is due. For example, Nicole's action point might be "I'll make a US map to use for the weather report we'll give on Thursday."

Copyright © 1998 LinguiSystems, Inc.

Interacts in Groups, *continued*

Individual Objectives

12. The student will problem solve in a group.

Classroom Activities

12. Over the course of a group activity, arrange several check-in points. Discuss how the work is going and areas where help may be needed. Teach students to keep focused on what needs to happen rather than on who isn't carrying their load.

Works Independently ···

1. The student will remain in his seat.

1. Give the student very specific directions about what to do during the activity and then when he's done. For example, the student may signal completion by turning his paper over and remaining quiet.

2. The student begins a task independently.

2. Structure the situation to allow the student maximum focus on the task. For example, if the student spends inordinate amounts of time gathering material and moving about the room, have materials in place ahead of time.

3. The student will work without distracting others.

3. Allow a range of choices conducive to concentrated seat work. A student may be seated near the teacher, in a study carrel, or at an individual desk rather than a table. As the student's behavior warrants, allow her more freedom to choose where she works.

4. The student will talk at appropriate times.

4. Teach the classroom rules for when it's appropriate to talk, such as raising your hand to participate in discussion or when not to talk, such as during a test.

5. The student can continue working through normal distractions.

5. Have students evaluate their own learning styles. Ask them to describe the best environment for working. Then, discuss how they can manage everyday distractions and still remain on task. Provide study carrels and quiet corners for students who need help blocking out auditory and visual stimuli.

Copyright © 1998 LinguiSystems, Inc.

Works Independently, *continued*

Individual Objectives	Classroom Activities

6. The student completes the assigned task.

6. Allow students time to check over their work for completion. Step by step, review what their work should include. Encourage any student needing more time to make arrangements with you. Students shouldn't be allowed to hand in partially completed assignments in an effort to teach them persistence and planning skills.

7. The student changes to another task or activity when told.

7. Tell students their current activity will end in two minutes, for example, so they have time to process and prepare for the upcoming change. Some students will need specific, consistent directions to get closure on the current activity before they change to the next one.

8. The student changes tasks or activities independently.

8. With the student, identify any teacher cues, such as "It's time to wrap up what we're doing" that signify the closing of one activity and getting ready for a new one. Since different teachers may have different cues, be sure to discuss cues for each teacher.

9. The student will volunteer for tasks.

9. Place a "volunteer pocket" on a bulletin board or attached to your desk. Include at least five tasks listed on individual index cards that can be selected each day. Tasks can range from taking attendance to the office, to being the first to answer a class discussion question. When a student completes his "volunteer work," write his name on the card and attach it to the bulletin board.

10. The student will seek teacher's attention appropriately.

10. Some students need specific teaching about when to approach a teacher and how to do it. As much as possible, have the student's teachers follow similar rules for recognition, such as raising your hand and awaiting a teacher's response before answering or approaching him.

Works Independently, *continued*

Individual Objectives

11. The student will focus on an assigned activity for ___ minutes.

12. The student will work on an activity or task with few on-task reminders.

13. The student will attend to an activity or task with no on-task reminders.

14. The student will finish a task or activity at an appropriate time.

15. The student will appropriately receive redirection and carry out correction of a completed task.

16. The student will monitor her own work quality and correct as needed.

17. The student will find another appropriate task or behavior when the first activity is done.

Classroom Activities

11. Give the student a kitchen timer to help regulate her on-task behavior. Gradually increase the time on task and provide rewards for doing so.

12. Provide specific limits and descriptors of behavior for a particular task. For example, a student working in pairs on an activity can be given the role of the recorder in the pair and reminded to look at and listen carefully to his partner. The student can be given two reminders, like "John, would you please focus on writing your partner's answers."

13. Before the student begins the task, tell her you won't be reminding her to stay on task — the responsibility is hers. Then, allow the student to receive the natural consequences of her completion or incompletion of work.

14. Provide students with models of acceptable work as well as reasonable time limits for completing it. Should a student need extended time, teach him to verbalize the need and time the request so it can be planned into the day's schedule or for the next day.

15. Teach the steps for handling feedback: hearing the person out and asking questions to clarify how to improve and what to do when a task is redone. Provide an example, such as correcting a math paper to show the steps rather than just writing the answer.

16. Build in a two-step process for grading work that rewards taking time for quality in addition to getting it done.

17. Place a center in the room for quiet activities to do when an activity is complete. Or have students take out their assignment books as a matter of routine when work is done to see what else to do.

Copyright © 1998 LinguiSystems, Inc.

Accepts Responsibility for Behavior ....

Individual Objectives

1. The student uses toys, books and materials in appropriate ways.

2. The student keeps desk or work area neat.

3. The student picks up when an activity is completed.

4. The student follows classroom rules of behavior without reminders.

5. The student asks for permission from a teacher or other person of authority.

6. The student will accept redirection from a teacher in a positive way.

Classroom Activities

1. Show students ways to handle a book or object before it's used. Remove the object should mishandling occur.

2. Establish a regular desk or work area check-in for students. The area can be checked at midmorning and then midafternoon so students only have necessary items on their desks.

3. Make sure directions are specific for what needs to be put away and how long it should take. Writing the time to be done on the board and listing items to be put away keeps students focused on the expected behavior.

4. Tape a list of classroom rules on the student's desk. Make sure the list specifically describes a behavior, such as "Raise your hand when you have something to say." Include only the rules the student needs to work on, particularly if he has already mastered other rules.

5. With students, make a poster listing situations in which they might need to ask permission to do something. For example, the teacher needs to be asked permission when a student needs to sharpen a pencil or use the bathroom. Role-play the correct way to ask and the need for timing the request during a pause in class activity. The teacher might say, "We have a few extra minutes. Now is a good time to ask to use the rest room or to have me check your work."

6. Inform other teachers who work with a student having this goal and share any strategies that have been successful. For example, a student may need redirection one-on-one in a private setting or in writing so she has a chance to absorb the feedback before acting on it.

Accepts Responsibility for Behavior, *continued*

Individual Objectives

7. The student will interact with teachers or other adults appropriately.

8. The student will accept responsibility for his own actions, including accepting praise or negative consequences.

9. The student will apologize when appropriate.

10. The student remembers and keeps an obligation.

11. The student will know when it's appropriate to take notes, instead of relying on memory.

Classroom Activities

7. Set up situations where the student can interact with adults and practice the more formal language used to talk to them. A student can volunteer to water plants in a teacher's room or to help out in the cafeteria before or after lunch.

8. A student's self-esteem can sometimes prevent her from accepting credit for an accomplishment or the consequences for a bad decision. When you become aware of situations, ask the student what decision she made that contributed to the outcome. Discuss what she has control of and how that worked in her favor. As needed, discuss how to rethink decisions with negative outcomes.

9. Create a variety of problem situations and print them up on index cards. Include several situations in which a student discovers he's in the wrong. In pairs, let students think of a solution and then rehearse what to say and do. Students can then present their role-plays to the class.

10. Discuss the importance of keeping obligations, respecting others' feelings and handling the consequences of a decision. Role-play situations depicting when obligations have or have not been kept and the positive, negative or realistic consequences of each.

11. Create a giant assignment book as a model. Then, make sure each student carries an assignment notebook including calendars. Whenever a due date is given for an assignment or returning library books, ask for a student volunteer to record the date in the giant book for future reference and have students put the information in their own individual assignment books.

Copyright © 1998 LinguiSystems, Inc.

Accepts Responsibility for Behavior, *continued*

Individual Objectives	Classroom Activities
12. The student will try to understand material before saying she doesn't understand it.	12. Let students "buddy up" to start assignments. First, have them read the directions together and then check each other for their understanding of the task. If students decide they need help, require them to ask a specific question indicating where they're experiencing trouble in understanding.
13. The student will let the teacher know when he's having trouble concentrating.	13. Teach students to verbalize what they need. Encourage students to identify the specific disruption, ask to be moved, or suggest a more conducive atmosphere for working, like the library or a study carrel.
14. The student will monitor the quality of her own work.	14. For any given individual assignment or activity, the student needs to learn to ask questions like "What is the assignment? Am I doing it?" and "How well have I done the activity?" A folder in which a student records self-evaluations of the quality given to assignments can help him monitor his pprogress and notice any patterns.
15. The student will accept and deal with frustration or disappointment.	15. Before situations that are potentially challenging for a student, let the student and a partner role-play appropriate ways to handle the situation. Let them also role-play ways that would aggravate the situation so they can compare solutions.
16. The student will put forth effort appropriate to the task.	16. Whether it's a class party they've volunteered for or a short-range assignment, students can benefit from preplanning sessions. Have students break down the steps needed for a project as well as estimating the time needed for each one. Then, on a monthly or weekly calendar, have students write which step to do which day, including the time estimate. As they complete each step, have them cross off the day.

Copyright © 1998 LinguiSystems, Inc.

Accepts Responsibility for Behavior, *continued*

Individual Objectives

17. The student will dress for P.E. class.

18. The student will participate in P.E. class.

19. The student will get to class on time.

20. The student will request help from the resource or regular education teacher.

Classroom Activities

17. First, discuss with the student and the parent, if needed, the source of the problem. If needed, make other arrangements for students to dress for P.E., like using the P.E. teacher's office or another empty classroom.

18. Some students may enjoy being "equipment managers" for the P.E. class so they have some sense of involvement. Also, encourage teachers to prearrange teams for team sports ahead of time so less socially adept students feel more at ease.

19. Arrange for students to make up time when they arrive late. For chronic problems, arrange for someone, like your consultant or school psychologist, to shadow the student to observe what behaviors are causing the tardiness, like socializing, locker problems or difficulties negotiating the hallways.

20. As an incentive for students to accept help, it may be necessary to develop a point system where students get points for participating in alternative arrangements. Points can then be used to boost scores on other tests or assignments if a teacher agrees to the arrangement.

Copyright © 1998 LinguiSystems, Inc.

Social Interaction and Communication

Marisa enters the room past the tardy bell, voice raised, and clearly out of control. Her locker has jammed, and a student in the hallway has made a negative remark. She stomps to her seat, slams her books on her desk, and gives me and her peers a look that says, "I dare you to add to my troubles." This sets the tone for the rest of the hour Marisa spends with her other LD peers in Learning Lab. Though it is a time set aside for help with academic work, today it becomes a battle-ground for working out the discrepancy between Marisa's perception of a situation and the need to put it into perspective and get on with the day.

Marisa does not perceive many situations like her regular education peers. Events are larger than life and her immature behaviors increase in magnitude correspondingly. What Marisa doesn't realize is that her handling of similar situations at school affects how others react to her socially. Consequently, Marisa puts off other students and her social life outside of school is not as rich and fulfilling as it could be.

Students like Marisa need help in perceiving, understanding and reacting to all of life's events. It is unfortunate, but for many students with learning disabilities, poorly developed social and communication skills can disable them more than their academic problems. The verbally adept, socially aware student with learning disabilities is the one who makes great strides in negotiating his way in the world.

The objectives and activities that follow will help your students develop essential skills for getting along well with others and succeeding in all areas of their lives.

- Uses Problem-solving Skills
- Shows Social Sensitivity
- Acts With Social Maturity
- Handles Conflict

Copyright © 1998 LinguiSystems, Inc.

Social Interaction and Communication

Yearly Goal: to develop skills for getting along well with others

Uses Problem-solving Skills ....

Individual Objectives

1. The student will learn words related to problem solving, like *conflict, solutions, alternatives,* and *compromise.*

2. The student will learn to think before acting.

3. The student will make an appointment with someone who can help solve the problem.

4. The student will respond calmly when faced with a problem.

Classroom Activities

1. Make a path board game with your students to practice problem-solving terminology. In the center of the board, label spots with the terminology you choose, like *conflicts, solutions, compromises*, and so on. Make cards with examples of these terms. When a player lands on a colored spot, she picks a card, labels the example, and then places it on the appropriate spot in the middle of the board. Eventually students could come up with their own example cards. Older students can be given cards related to other areas, like careers, employment, dating, or parent problems.

2. At the start of a school year or semester, it's a good idea to make classroom rules clear. To help clarify and practice following the rules, create various scenarios, either following or not following the rules. Then, have students think before they react to each scenario. Create scenarios for outside the classroom, too.

3. Provide students with sample problems that need to be solved. Have them brainstorm appropriate people to be resources. Then, rehearse setting up an appointment and consulting with the individual.

4. Practice some biofeedback techniques with your students. Have students analyze what physical and emotional symptoms indicate they're "losing control," like raising their voices or feeling like they'll say something they'll regret. Have them come up with individual ways to get think and pause time before they react.

Copyright © 1998 LinguiSystems, Inc.

Uses Problem-solving Skills, *continued*

Individual Objectives

5. The student will provide convincing reasons for a belief.

6. The student will work out a conflict with a peer.

7. The student will recognize what he has control over.

8. The student will learn ways to adapt to change or surprises.

9. The student will take responsibility for and learn from mistakes.

10. The student will learn time management techniques.

Classroom Activities

5. Give students problem-solving situations related to school, home and the community. Have them role-play their positions on the situation providing two convincing reasons as support. Older students can discuss and debate the role of being convincing as it relates to careers like sales and the law.

6. Provide a private place for students to talk with one another. Give students the option to have you or another adult there to help problem solve.

7. Have students take a commercially-prepared inventory to help them determine their locus of control. (*Life Works* [1]) Or create a variety of scenarios and discuss who's in control of the situation and how it can be handled.

8. Prepare students for changes, such as a change in the daily schedule for a special event, when a substitute will be teaching, or when a scheduled visit to a parent is postponed. Arrange for an individual check-in meeting so the student can share her feelings and reactions. Discuss how the situation can be handled positively.

9. Share literature and magazine or news articles describing other people's personal trials and tribulations. *Reader's Digest* is a great source for human interest stories of all ages. Discuss how these individuals have grown and benefited from their mistakes.

10. Teach students how to plan their time to avoid potential problems in any area of their lives. Have them keep a time chart assessing how they are currently spending their time. Then, have them evaluate the chart in terms of how their time commitments match their personal priorities and values. Together, plan simple ways to gain the time to do what they'd most like to do.

[1] Dalke, Connie and Howard, Diane. *Life Works: A Transition Program for High School Students.* East Moline, IL: LinguiSystems, Inc., 1994.

Uses Problem-solving Skills, *continued*

Individual Objectives	**Classroom Activities**
11. The student will set and prioritize goals.	11. Have students set and prioritize their goals for a day or two and try to remain committed to them. Then, have them handle a day spontaneously, reacting to things as they come up. Let them discuss or journal write about their feelings in comparing the two situations.
12. The student will learn to set realistic goals.	12. Setting realistic goals requires a student to evaluate his own abilities, his ability to make a commitment, and any time, energy or resource constraints. Discuss students' goals often and challenge honestly how realistic their thinking is.

Shows Social Sensitivity ···

1. The student will recognize facial expressions.	1. Use a variety of ways to help students interpret feelings and meanings behind facial expressions. Look at pictures, videos of TV dramas, or even videos of students interacting in a classroom. Turn the sound off so students can practice just the one skill. Then, show the video with accompanying conversation.
2. The student will smile when smiled at.	2. Brainstorm with the student things that make her happy, like receiving praise for a good job, earning a privilege or being greeted by a friend. Then, role-play the dialogue and body language, like smiling, that would be part of the interaction.
3. The student will learn how to make friends.	3. For some students, you may need to prearrange experiences in which they have the opportunity to make a friend. An after-school bowling or video game trip, or a play date made through arrangement with another student's parent may facilitate making friends.

Copyright © 1998 LinguiSystems, Inc.

Shows Social Sensitivity, *continued*

Individual Objectives

4. The student will understand common gestures.

5. The student will recognize the meaning of tones of voice.

6. The student will learn how to gain peers' attention appropriately.

7. The student will learn how to be an active or empathic listener.

8. The student will understand the importance of and practice good manners.

9. The student will learn to express appreciativeness.

Classroom Activities

4. Teach students common gestures used in a variety of situations, like thumbs up, a finger held against the lips, palms up with a shoulder shrug, and so on. Have fun brainstorming. On a wall chart, draw gestures and their meanings. Discuss the situations under which the gestures are most appropriate.

5. Make an audiotape having various people role-play reacting to a variety of situations. Then, have students interpret the feelings conveyed by the tones of voices they hear.

6. Talk about the concept of personal space; how some people are more comfortable with contact or close proximity than others. Then, with willing peers, practice how they prefer to be approached and how much contact, like a pat on the back or a handshake, is comfortable to them.

7. Either with the teacher or another student, have a short discussion about something you care about, like a favorite pet, a fun experience, or a time you helped a friend. Have the student then paraphrase what you said, including your feelings about the experience to show he was actively listening. Then, reverse roles.

8. Create a polite atmosphere in your classroom. Follow classroom rules, like saying "Thank you" when you or a peer helps a student, asking "May I please get a drink?" when requesting to leave the classroom, or responding "Thank you for controlling your temper" when a student maintains control.

9. As a class, think of people who have done something for you lately. Talk about how to appropriately express appreciativeness, like with a thank-you, a short note or even a smile. Then, encourage thanking each other in the classroom for various things peers do.

Copyright © 1998 LinguiSystems, Inc.

Individual Objectives

Classroom Activities

10. The student will learn how to join a group.

10. Teach students common phrases for making a request to join, such as "Hey, is it okay if I join in?" or "What are you doing? Could you use another team member?"

11. The student will learn how to give a compliment.

11. Play any one of the commercial social skills games (e.g., *FriendZee* [1]) that includes compliment giving. Then, encourage giving genuine compliments to peers when they are deserved.

12. The student will learn how to greet others.

12. Model how to greet others by greeting each student as she enters the room. Stress eye contact and being in proximity to the person. Make it a rule that the student needs to greet two other people later that day.

13. The student will know how to introduce himself.

13. Any time students enter a new situation, from first being in your classroom to going on field trips, encourage them to introduce themselves to others. In addition to their names, they should include a descriptive phrase about themselves related to the situation, such as "Hi, I'm Cliff. I've been to the Cincinnati Zoo before. Do you have jaguars here, too?"

14. The student will share conversation time and regulate own amount of talking.

14. Arrange a set time a few times a week for the student to have an informal conversation with a small group. Lay the ground rules for turn taking and listening to others ahead of time.

Acts with Social Maturity ···

1. The student will be a good sport in an activity or game.

1. Make sure the student understands and can explain back to you the rules for a game or activity. Include the expected behavior for turn taking and the appropriate way to react to winning or losing the game.

[1] Figula, Diane. *FriendZee: A Social Skills Game.* East Moline, IL: LinguiSystems, Inc., 1992.

                    Copyright © 1998 LinguiSystems, Inc.

Individual Objectives

Classroom Activities

2. The student will work in a group.

2. Start with a small group of two students. Have the students complete a structured activity together, like a class assignment. Allow the students to work together frequently so they become comfortable with each other. Later, expand the group to three students and have them work on a variety of activities.

3. The student will do things independently within the school setting.

3. Before turning a student loose on his own, accompany him yourself or send a competent peer for a trial run. Then, review what he's to do and send him on his own. Make sure requests are legitimate, such as sending him to the library to pick out books for the library corner.

4. The student will make a purchase independently.

4. Encourage parents to provide the student with a small allowance. Then, either at a school store, during a class field trip or with her parents, allow the student to plan and make a purchase.

5. The student will go places independently.

5. Work with the student's parents on goals for independence. For a younger student, it may be arranging a get-together with a friend and then walking to the friend's house. For an older student, it can be taking the bus to school or work. Encourage parents to go on trial runs and talk through the situation with their child.

6. The student will make and carry out a plan.

6. Allow students to plan for major events in the classroom. For example, on parents' day or prior to an open house, students can plan and make invitations, decide on work to show, things to include on the bulletin board, and refreshments to serve. Encourage parents to allow their children to make and carry out plans at home, such as preparing for supper or for a special visitor.

Copyright © 1998 LinguiSystems, Inc.

Acts with Social Maturity, *continued*

Individual Objectives

7. The student will consider the social consequences of his behavior.

8. The student will use good judgment in making decisions.

9. The student will persevere with a task.

10. The student will control reactions to a frustrating situation.

11. The student will understand the appropriate time and place for certain behavior and actions.

12. The student will perform in front of a group.

Classroom Activities

7. At times, students find it hard to think beyond their immediate needs and feelings. Encourage students to think through how their peers will react to their words or actions. Through discussion or role-playing, have students experience seeing things from another's perspective.

8. Teach the student the steps for making a good decision: weighing the pros and cons, evaluating time and material needed, and evaluating the possible outcomes. Provide many potential scenarios for practice.

9. Prearrange a break time for the student in the midst of a difficult task. Set the break time at a logical point in the task so the student can see a concrete accomplishment before continuing on.

10. Handling frustration by crumpling an assignment paper or a vocal outburst interrupts everyone's work needlessly. Defuse the situation with humor. Remind the student by asking her an absurd question or by making an exaggerated comment about the situation. For example, you might say, "Well, I think we'll have to cancel all written work for the rest of the week" when a student temporarily loses a favorite pen. Humor can help students put their own frustrations into perspective.

11. Have students make books detailing behavior and actions for certain situations. Students can illustrate the book and list guidelines for behavior, such as picking up after oneself in the cafeteria, remaining quiet during classroom directions and work time, or being good sports during gym time.

12. Allow students to use index cards for notes and props, like posters or relevant objects to help give them confidence during presentations.

Copyright © 1998 LinguiSystems, Inc.

Acts with Social Maturity, *continued*

Individual Objectives	Classroom Activities
13. The student will try new things and experiences.	13. Create new experiences frequently. Students can choose to try a new food, attempt an activity or interact with a new person. Students can keep a journal about their experiences to share with you.
14. The student will learn how to help others.	14. On index cards, create a variety of real-life in and out of school situations. When students finish an assignment, they can grab a problem-solving card and plan a solution. Have the student write his ideas or schedule a sharing time with you.
15. The student will learn how to be friendly to others.	15. Have students think of questions to ask a peer they'd like to get to know better. Allow students to work together on an assignment so they can apply the skills as they work.
16. The student will recognize appropriate times and situations to approach others.	16. Students need to recognize that the timing and situation surrounding their actions affect the results. Brainstorm times when you would or would not approach people like a teacher, a parent, a friend, or a sibling for help or a favor. Discuss times when they were involved in situations in which another person reacted in an unexpected way due to timing or the situation.
17. The student will understand jokes and other social humor.	17. Teach students common figurative expressions and regional colloquialisms so they understand the humor in jokes and humorous situations.
18. The student will participate in activities similar to peers, like league or intramural sports, or a job after school.	18. Students expand social and communication skills by expanding the arena in which they practice them. Arrange with parents to have students increase their outside activities if they aren't already doing so. Pave the way for the student by talking to the coach or employer ahead of time about the student's needs and abilities.

Copyright © 1998 LinguiSystems, Inc.

Handles Conflict

Individual Objectives

1. The student will express negative feelings appropriately, like displeasure or frustration.

2. The student will apologize appropriately.

3. The student will ignore teasing, name calling or other negative comments.

4. The student will leave anger-causing situations.

5. The student will express anger with non-aggressive words.

Classroom Activities

1. Many students don't realize the impact of their word choices when expressing feelings. Word choices can affect peer relationships as well as school consequences for their behavior. Give students more appropriate words to use, such as saying "I'm angry because you won't listen to me," instead of saying "You're stupid" while shoving the student away. Wall posters reminding students how to express common feelings can be helpful.

2. Praise apologies when they occur. Also, model apologies to your students when you make a mistake or forget something they asked you to do. Reinforce the behavior by role-playing other home or social situations in which an apology may be appropriate.

3. Praise students who don't succumb to the cruelty of peers. Then, allow the student to express privately to you how the other student's words made her feel. Talk about any of her behaviors that may have provoked the other student. Then, discuss how she can handle the next difficult situation.

4. Allow the student to request a time-out when he feels anger may overwhelm him. Getting a drink or having a quick chat with a favorite school employee may help the student cool down and rethink how he wants to react.

5. Teach the student how to make "I messages," describing how she feels. Provide a private place for the student to vent or to work out a conflict with a peer.

Copyright © 1998 LinguiSystems, Inc.

Handles Conflict, *continued*

Individual Objectives	**Classroom Activities**
6. The student will take constructive criticism or redirection.	6. Find out ahead of time how the student best handles constructive criticism by asking him yourself. Since the student will have social skills he'll be working on, an open discussion about what you'll be working on together and how redirection will occur will smooth the way for progress.
7. The student will respond to punishment or behavioral consequences appropriately.	7. Wait to deliver and enforce consequences until the student is ready to listen and control her reactions. Then, show the student in concrete terms the consequences for her behavior. You might write the expected rule followed with a description of consequences. Or if the consequence is the loss of a privilege for a given period of time, record on a calendar when the privilege resumes.

Copyright © 1998 LinguiSystems, Inc.

Transition to the Real World

I teach a Transitions class for my high school students because I believe transition issues can truly be addressed only if purposeful time is set aside for them. As much as we and our regular education colleagues would like to think we help students plan for their futures within our day-to-day curriculum, in reality, we're scrambling to cover the basics and, when we can, make some connection to the future.

Aaron, Tony, Michelle, Serena, Chad, and Jared, members of the Transition Class of '97, have changed my perceptions about how students with learning disabilities need to meet their futures. My initial approach to this year's Transition class was to cover key units and concepts together as a class.

Geared with a wonderful predesigned curriculum that would eliminate the time-consuming search for materials, I set out to cover everything this year's students would need. For six weeks we filled out interest and skill inventories, immersed ourselves in discussions of values, and read stories promoting key beliefs that guarantee a "successful" future for everyone. In short, we were using a prepackaged IEP plan designed to fit everyone and fitting no one. The ideas were sound, but they didn't inspire my students, and I didn't feel right about what I was doing. So, I scrapped $300 worth of truly wonderful materials in favor of a workshop approach to transition with two key components:

- goals that I felt were absolutely essential for a good quality of life, like managing money well, knowing how to use time, applying and interviewing for a job, and most importantly, having dreams and goals that give direction to their lives.

- opportunities for student decision-making that would happen every hour they spent in my class. From planning their weekly or daily calendar of activities, to deciding how to act in class that day, to making arrangements for a job shadow experience, my students would be put in charge.

Turning over the class to my students has provided them with their greatest resource — themselves. After all, there is no "resource room" in real life. As "graduates," I hope Michelle, Serena, Tony, Chad, Aaron, and Jared leave Transition Class '97 equipped with:

- decision-making skills that will equip them to deal with seemingly insignificant daily goals to grandiose dreams of the future

- a realistic knowledge of their skills and abilities, and a clear vision of their potential and dreams

- social and communication skills that will allow them to articulate their needs, interests and goals

- daily living skills like banking, budgeting and job skills that will ensure them quality lifestyles

The IEP objectives that follow will help your "graduates" meet goals in their whole lives — personal, social, educational, and financial — by strengthening abilities in the following areas:

- Self-Advocacy
- Career Awareness
- Workplace Readiness
- Everyday Living Skills

Copyright © 1998 LinguiSystems, Inc.

Transition to the Real World

Yearly Goal: to prepare for future needs

Self-Advocacy

Recognizes Academic & Personal Needs ·······································

Individual Objectives

1. The student will know her learning styles.

2. The student will verbalize learning deficit areas as well as learning strengths.

3. The student will practice time-management strategies.

4. The student will set and meet short- and long-range goals.

Classroom Activities

1. Have students take a variety of commercially-prepared learning style inventories. Then, have students make posters or summarize in a speech what they learned about their learning styles.

2. Students should summarize their deficit areas and learning strengths by reviewing their cumulative folders for past academic history, grade reports and psychological reports documenting their special ed placement.

3. Given time logs, have students record hour by hour use of time daily and on the weekends. Then, have them review the information and set time lines for accomplishing goals.

4. Create planning sheets for short- and long-range goals. Then, have students periodically set short- and long-range goals. For each goal, students should list steps to meet it including a time line and resources. Review your students' goals and plans with them. After goals are met or not met, have students record their feelings and reactions in a journal.

Copyright © 1998 LinguiSystems, Inc.

Self-Advocacy, *continued*

Individual Objectives	Classroom Activities
5. The student will follow through on daily and long-term commitments.	5. Any young person has difficulty focusing on more than the next minute, and the student with a learning disability even more so. Meet frequently with these students to work on communication skills that affect their personal, social, work, and academic lives. Rehearse skills, such as saying "no" to a commitment she really doesn't want to make or getting back to someone she promised to get information to.
6. The student will recognize personal symptoms of frustration.	6. Have students keep daily journals of feelings, noting when they feel comfortable in a situation and when they're frustrated. Use the journals to problem solve difficult situations.
7. The student will identify what motivates her success.	7. Finishing school as well as succeeding with a career takes motivation. Invite former students who dropped out of school but eventually finished their educations to speak to your students. Your students may also enjoy reading inspirational literature or listening to motivational tapes.

Seeks Accommodations

Individual Objectives	Classroom Activities
1. The student will explain disability and needs.	1. Have students rehearse with the resource teacher how they'll explain their disability and needs. Then, have students select and approach teachers who most need to know about them. Students can practice strategies for approaching co-workers and employees, too.
2. The student will assess his need for accommodations.	2. Encourage each student to make up a list of accommodations appropriate to his needs. For example, students could request copies of teacher notes if they have writing or processing problems, or they might ask for tests to be read aloud in the case of reading needs. (See Accommodations, pages 166-167, for more ideas.)

Self-Advocacy, *continued*

Individual Objectives

3. The student will ask for accommodations.

4. The student will adjust need for accommodations to a particular course, teacher, test, or assignment.

5. The student will lead own IEP agenda.

6. The student will learn to discuss accommodations on the job.

Classroom Activities

3. For each course, students should predict their needs depending on things like course content or instructor's teaching style. Then, either at the beginning of the course or as needed, students negotiate accommodations with their teachers.

4. Students may not need accommodations for every assignment they do or test they take. Have students look at their assignment notebooks to project when the next accommodation will be needed for an individual test or assignment. Then, the student should meet with the teacher after class at least two or more days before the assignment or test.

5. As students near graduation, it's important for them to take as much control as possible for their educational planning, especially if they're considering post-secondary schooling. With the student, plan an agenda for the IEP meeting. Have the student gather information about her academic progress and other needed information. Then, have the student determine the meeting date and invite her team members. Rehearse with the student how to open and guide the meeting.

6. By law, students can also seek accommodations from their employers. Have students list the job duties they perform. Then, discuss any accommodations they need to help them perform more effectively. For example, a student may need an employer to leave audio-taped instructions rather than instructions to read.

Career Awareness

Identifies Skills, Interests and Aptitudes ....

1. The student will identify own skills and abilities.

1. Let students review their cumulative folders, their grade reports and psychological reports to determine skill strengths and abilities.

Individual Objectives

Classroom Activities

2. The student will recognize interests and relevance to careers.

2. Have students schedule appointments with their guidance counselors or a career counselor to review their skills and interests and get career information related to potential careers.

3. The student will evaluate aptitudes to help make career choices.

3. Arrange for students to take commercially-prepared aptitude inventories. Many community colleges also provide career counseling and testing services for interested students.

4. The student will narrow career choices to fit personality and needs.

4. Have students write the ideal job description. They should include the job setting, duties, pay, and perks. Then, have students match the job description with two to three real-life careers they can continue to explore.

Researches Post-secondary Options

1. The student will determine desired lifestyle.

1. As a project, have students list future wants, like an apartment, a car, a high paying job, a wife/husband and children, free time for personal interests, and so on. Then, ask students to put a "price" on their lifestyle and plan what they need to do to reach lifetime goals.

2. The student will research career possibilities.

2. Using library, guidance office, and Internet resources, have students research and report on careers. Reports should include education, interests, skills needed, job duties, and salary possibilities.

3. The student will use community resources to explore career options.

3. Set up "job shadowing" opportunities for students with several community people ranging from minimum wage positions to manufacturing jobs to professional positions. Have students decide if they'd like the job, and what skills, interests and education it would take to get it.

Transition to the Real World
The LD Teacher's IEP Companion
153
Copyright © 1998 LinguiSystems, Inc.

Individual Objectives

Classroom Activities

4. The student will seek information from local colleges about available programs.

4. Have students write letters of inquiry to local colleges seeking college catalogs and potential campus visits. Then, have each student develop a chart to record information comparing and contrasting various college offerings.

5. The student will complete a college application.

5. Have students create personal data sheets of information likely to be asked about on a college application, including personal, educational and financial information. Then, have students practice filling out an actual application for a local community college and explain the admission process.

6. The student will make arrangements to take skill assessment tests.

6. In addition to or in place of SAT and ACT test scores, many colleges screen applicants by way of skill assessment tests in areas like reading, writing and math. Take students to visit a local community college to find out about the tests and the admissions process. Have students take the tests, if possible, as a way to measure their potential for college coursework.

7. The student will learn about Section 504 of the Rehabilitation Act of 1973 and its impact on college accommodations.

7. Make sure students understand that, unlike in the public schools, they are responsible for seeking accommodations once they enter a post-secondary institution. When the post-secondary institution is aware of the student's needs, it legally must provide "reasonable" accommodations.

8. The student will increase awareness of supportive employment or postsecondary education opportunities through local vocational rehabilitation agencies.

8. Encourage each student to contact and set up an appointment with an area vocational rehabilitation counselor. At that time, the student can share future goals.

Acquires Important Occupational Skills

1. The student will take coursework to explore and learn skills in a possible future occupation.

1. As early as eighth and ninth grades, have students meet with their guidance counselors to choose courses that will expose them to different occupations and skills. Students can take courses in areas like business, health services, building and trades, or engineering.

Individual Objectives

2. The student will explore career options through hands-on experience.

3. The student will participate in extracurricular activities as part of career exploration.

4. The student will use current technology like computers, CD Roms, calculators, and CAD equipment.

Classroom Activities

2. Through job shadowing, internships and business partnerships, set up field trips and experiences for students to sample a variety of career options. If a student likes a particular experience, develop the situation into onsite training or potential employment.

3. Counsel individual students to explore extracurricular activities that might help develop skills. For example, volunteering to referee youth games might be useful for a career in sports and recreation, or being the business manager for the school newspaper could develop skills for a business, sales or marketing job.

4. As part of a student's career exploration and preparation, she should explore the type of technology currently used within her field of interest. Then, arrange hands-on experiences within your school or at local businesses for students to learn more about technology.

Workplace Readiness

Looks for a Job

1. The student can read newspaper, TV or online want ads.

2. The student will assess job availability in the area.

1. Students can make a chart to record information they get from want ads. The chart should include employer's name, address and phone, category and description of job, hours, and salary. After reading several ads, have students compare what they learn.

2. Students should meet with and interview an employment counselor to assess types of jobs available in your community.

Copyright © 1998 LinguiSystems, Inc.

Individual Objectives	**Classroom Activities**
3. The student will evaluate personal areas of job or career interest.	3. There are many commercial interest inventories available for students to assess their interests. Your guidance office or a local community college's career counseling office may also offer computerized versions of inventories. Arrange for students to take a couple of inventories to compare results and then follow up with career counseling.
4. The student will participate in on-site job shadowing and observation.	4. Arrange several short-term job shadowing experiences for students. Prepare students ahead of time on how to act, what things to observe and how to analyze the experience afterwards. Ask employees observed to give students feedback, too, depending on any hands-on experience they had during the shadowing.
5. The student will learn about apprenticeship opportunities.	5. For students interested in fields like plumbing, electrical contracting or carpentry, arrange for local organizations to explain their apprenticeship programs. Students need to be aware of training and pay as well as the types of commitments required of them to participate in an apprenticeship.

Applies and Interviews for a Job

1. The student will fill out a job application accurately.	1. Get applications from several different types of employers. Then, have students fill out applications, adapting their information to the types of employment offered.
2. The student will write a business resume.	2. Teach students the computer skills for producing a professional-looking resume. When students are done, invite actual employers to review and give feedback on the resumes.
3. The student will write a business letter requesting job information.	3. Provide students with several examples of actual business letters and review what's included. Then, have students write and send business letters to local employers seeking job information.

Individual Objectives

Classroom Activities

4. The student will become aware of rights to be respected during an interview.

4. Because your students have disabilities, it's very important to inform them about questions that an employer may or may not ask during an interview. Discuss why some questions may not be asked in relationship to potential discrimination.

5. The student will contact a potential employer by phone or in writing to set up an interview.

5. Role-play phone calls between students and an "employer." Stress the importance of speaking clearly and communicating in a professional manner. Then, have students make actual phone calls.

6. The student will learn personal skills for showing interest and enthusiasm.

6. Students often don't know how they come across to other people. Often times, interest and enthusiasm can be "masked" because of the newness of a situation. Role-play and videotape practice interviews with these students. Then, very sensitively, coach students with specific feedback to help them present their best selves to a potential employer.

7. The student will follow up on an interview.

7. Rehearse and role-play with students how to follow up on an interview by thanking the employer and also by checking current employability status. Stress the importance of follow-up to show the employer strong interest in the job.

8. The student will write a thank-you letter.

8. Encourage students to send thank-you letters to prospective employers to thank them for the interview experience. The letter should review the points discussed during the interview and also let the employer know the student is still interested.

Interacts Appropriately with Co-workers and Customers ·······································

1. The student will work in a team to complete a task.

1. In a classroom setting, give students a variety of experiences working in teams. Give group assignments where the team plans the *how* and *who* of accomplishing them. Or let groups plan and arrange for outside activities, speakers and field trips instead of you.

Transition to the Real World
The LD Teacher's IEP Companion   157   Copyright © 1998 LinguiSystems, Inc.

Individual Objectives

Classroom Activities

2. The student will get work done on time.

2. Provide students with a variety of real-life job scenarios in which they must plan how to get a given job done on time. For example, a roofer may need to put a roof on a new house or a salesclerk may need to have items priced before a huge sale. Have students list steps including the planning and communication necessary to ensure a timely and complete job. You can also encourage punctuality and dependability by assigning part of a grade to these features any time you give a classroom assignment.

3. The student will communicate in a professional way.

3. Invite a personnel director or human resources manager from a local company to speak on job communication issues like sexual harassment or rumor spreading. Encourage students to model professional communication within your classroom, too.

4. The student will deal with problems in a polite manner.

4. Have students make up and then role-play a variety of situations that may occur with customers and between co-workers. Video-tape students role-playing appropriate and inappropriate ways of handling situations. Follow up by making posters of rules or tips for getting along.

5. The student will be helpful to co-workers.

5. Take an inventory of jobs currently held by your students. For each job, have students list how someone else could help them do their job faster, easier or more completely. Then, have them consider a co-worker's job and make the same kind of list. Discuss the benefits to everyone of "pitching in."

6. The student will demonstrate sensitivity to people of varying backgrounds.

6. Hold a weekly current events discussion to discuss how people's backgrounds affect job interaction. Students should bring in news from a newspaper, magazine or a TV/radio broadcast that deals with issues like the plight of migrant workers or issues of working parents.

Individual Objectives

Classroom Activities

7. The student will express feelings, reactions and ideas in an appropriate manner.

7. In individual counseling sessions, discuss with students areas for growth. Have students set one or two major goals, like "I'll listen to others before giving my opinion" or "I'll ask for help when I'm feeling frustrated." Have students monitor progress by keeping a weekly "interaction log" or meeting periodically for feedback from you.

8. The student can remember or record important information from a phone call or other customer contact.

8. Make an audiotape of "customers" at a variety of businesses. Have students practice taking notes or summarizing important information to relay to another co-worker. After each customer, have student pairs compare notes.

9. The student will keep boss and co-workers informed of things like need for schedule changes and important customer information.

9. Before a student takes a job, the employer should share with him the purpose of the business he'll work for and how his role affects the roles of others. For example, the receptionist in a hair salon schedules timely appointments for customers that consequently affect the work schedules of the stylists. Not showing up for work causes the stylists to give customers poorer service and may result in the loss of business.

Practices Job-keeping Skills ·······································

1. The student will have good attendance on the job.

1. Have each student worker make a copy of her weekly or monthly schedule and then record each day actually worked. For any day missed, she must write down why and follow it up with a conversation with her employer or work-experience coordinator. Review the record periodically.

2. The student will be on time to work each day.

2. On a time sheet divided into quarter hours, students should list what they're to do prior to actually being at work. Time should be allotted for things like showering, choosing clothes, using transportation, and any unexpected interruptions.

Individual Objectives

3. The student will respect and listen to superiors.

4. The student will follow rules of the workplace.

5. The student will accept responsibility for successes as well as mistakes on the job.

6. The student will be organized on the job.

7. The student will balance work, school and personal life.

Classroom Activities

3. List the types of responsibilities bosses usually assign to employees. Discuss why these responsibilities are important to follow through on. Also, make up example situations to problem solve times when a worker might be tempted to disrespect bosses' orders, but should either follow them anyway or negotiate with the boss.

4. The student should write the basic rules of the workplace on an index card. Then, she should review the list with her employer to confirm her understanding of the rules.

5. Teach your students to accept responsibility and apologize when they make a mistake on a job. More importantly, help them understand that they need to ask their employer questions ahead of time as well as after the incident to learn from their experiences. When you have the opportunity, model the skills for your students or share tough experiences from your past work history.

6. Competent workers have both the ability to manage time to complete a job and the ability to find the materials like tools or necessary papers to do it. Encourage students to write to-do lists prioritizing what they need to do on the job. You may also want to visit the job site to see how students organize the materials and place in which they work to be most efficient.

7. Have students use calendars and planners for scheduling things they need to do in their daily lives. Taking the time to record a daily schedule of work hours, school hours and leisure hours can help students make better decisions.

Transition to the Real World
The LD Teacher's IEP Companion

160

Copyright © 1998 LinguiSystems, Inc.

Everyday Living Skills

Understands and Manages Money Well ....

Individual Objectives

1. The student can make a personal budget.

2. The student will understand the use of credit cards and loans.

3. The student will calculate the sale price of an item.

4. The student will understand the importance of keeping receipts and warranties.

5. The student will comparison shop at grocery stores.

6. The student will read and pay a bill.

Classroom Activities

1. Have students imagine they're living on their own five years from now. Let them brainstorm all the expenses they'll have as well as project their income. Then, provide monthly budget sheets so students can itemize and plan for expenses.

2. Bring in a speaker from a local bank to talk about the advantages and disadvantages of credit cards and loans.

3. Review converting percent off and fractions like 1/2 off to decimals. Using real ads or a trip to the mall, have students figure sale prices of given items. Have them compare sale prices of similar items and choose the better buy.

4. Create problem-solving situations for students to role-play. Have situations involve things like products that break before the warranty expires, items that don't fit or car repairs that weren't satisfactory.

5. Let students plan a typical weekly menu for one person who would prepare most meals at home. Allot students a reasonable amount of money, allowing for one or two meals eaten out. Then, bring in ads and have students make grocery lists and itemize the costs to stay within budget.

6. Bring in samples of bills like gas, electric, phone, and car. Use a highlighter to point out important information like the due date, the actual payment and any interest. Discuss what happens as a result of late or nonpayment.

Copyright © 1998 LinguiSystems, Inc.

Individual Objectives   **Classroom Activities**

7. The student can write a check and record the transaction.

7. With a sample checkbook from a local bank, create purchasing situations for students. As they make purchases, they must write checks accurately, record the amounts and keep a running balance in their checkbooks.

8. The student will investigate and secure a checking account.

8. Review with students checking account options, like combination checking and savings accounts or checking accounts requiring minimum balances. Then, have students visit banks, talk to bank personnel and obtain printed material about accounts. Students can then make a chart comparing accounts to help them make a final decision.

9. The student will make an ATM transaction.

9. As part of investigating checking account and savings options, arrange for a bank employee to demonstrate ATM transactions. Stress the possible fees for such transactions and the need to maintain accurate personal records.

10. The student will fill out a simple tax form.

10. Get actual tax forms from your local IRS office, library or post office. Then, provide students with simulated pay check stubs as well as W-2 forms to use for filling out the form. Discuss or demonstrate the electronic process being used by phone, also.

Finds Own Transportation

1. The student will get self to and from school, work or other places.

1. One real step toward independence is for a student to predict and plan for transportation needs. Encourage parents to let students make their own transportation arrangements. For example, if the student needs to arrive earlier than usual to school, she must request the special arrangement with her parent for the ride. If the ride is not available, she has to explore other options.

Individual Objectives

2. The student will read a bus or subway schedule.

3. The student will use the local bus or subway.

4. The student will explore the purchase of a car.

5. The student will understand car insurance options.

Classroom Activities

2. Make copies of actual bus or subway schedules for your community. Give students simulated scenarios, such as getting to and from work on the opposite side of town. Let them highlight the schedule they'd follow to plan the most efficient travel routes.

3. Arrange for a parent, a teacher aide or yourself to make trial run-throughs with the student using the bus or subway. When the student knows the procedure and the route, allow her to make the trip independently.

4. From budgeting to visiting the dealership, brainstorm all the steps to follow in buying a car. Then, have students choose a dream car and plan the steps for buying it. Let students role-play the interactions that are part of the process, such as calling about insurance or negotiating with the dealer.

5. Teach students car insurance terms ahead of time like *liability insurance*, *deductible*, and *premium*. As a class, research and select a car to "buy." Then, invite different car insurance agents at different times to speak to students about different insurance plans available for the car. Have the speakers stress good student discounts and good driving records as options for keeping premiums low.

Cares for Self and Home

1. The student will do his own laundry.

2. The student will plan and cook meals.

1. Have the student bring in a duffel bag of his own laundry. Then, using either school facilities or a local laundromat, demonstrate how to do laundry. Encourage parents to expect the student to do his own laundry once he knows how.

2. Encourage students to take a cooking class or an independent living class so they learn cooking basics. Or arrange for parents to help the student prepare a simple meal each week for his family.

Copyright © 1998 LinguiSystems, Inc.

Individual Objectives	**Classroom Activities**
3. The student will have an appropriate appearance for school or work.	3. For some students, it may be necessary to review the rules of good hygiene. Discuss how cleanliness and appearance affect social and work opportunities. Some students may need special arrangements made, like showering at school, to facilitate good grooming and clothing care.
4. The student will understand and practice personal safety.	4. Discuss and problem solve situations requiring caution, like keeping doors locked and not walking alone at night. Have a speaker from your local police department discuss issues of personal safety and methods of protection.
5. The student will handle emergency situations.	5. Encourage students to take a first-aid class offered by your local Red Cross or another agency. Or arrange for speakers and videos to review the basics of first-aid. Discuss preventing emergencies by keeping the home and workplace safe.
6. The student will plan leisure and recreational activities.	6. Have students research community options for leisure and recreation. Then, let students design pamphlets, categorizing activities by criteria like price or type of activity. Students should include addresses, phone numbers and other contact information.
7. The student will explore future housing arrangements.	7. Have teams of students research housing arrangements in your community. One team can explore costs, advantages and disadvantages of apartment dwelling, while another team can explore renting or owning a house. Also, consider housing costs for students who may decide to attend college. Compare information with continuing to live at home or with a relative.

Copyright © 1998 LinguiSystems, Inc.

Individual Objectives

8. The student will match personal needs with community resources.

Classroom Activities

8. Get brochures from local agencies that detail services for local citizens as well as individuals with disabilities. Have students make and laminate a quick reference list of the agencies and phone numbers to keep by their phones. A list might look like this:

Agency	Purpose	Phone No.
Voc Rehab	for job placement and training	555-3879
Advocacy Group	support for other people with disabilities	555-8742
Adult Ed	furthering career skills, exploring hobbies	555-0912
Community Health Services	low-cost medical treatment	555-7594
Legal Aid	legal service for low income individuals	555-0090

Copyright © 1998 LinguiSystems, Inc.

Accommodations in the Regular Classroom

Student's Name _____

Grade _____

IEP Date _____

Check each item that should be considered in planning the student's IEP.

Environmental Strategies

❏ providing preferential seating

❏ using study carrels for isolation

❏ providing time-out opportunities

❏ pairing with another student who helps write or read

❏ providing adaptive equipment or furniture, like access to a computer, a tape recorder, or study carrel (specify: _____)

❏ taking special field trips or having guest speakers

❏ structuring the environment to reduce stress on the student

❏ using community resources

Motivational Strategies

❏ sending home regular progress reports

❏ immediate reinforcement or consequences

❏ keeping charts of student's progress

❏ student reading lesson to aide, peer tutor or teacher

❏ school-to-home communication system

❏ contract with the teacher

❏ peer teaching opportunities

❏ pretesting and post-testing for mastery

❏ daily assignment sheet or notebook

Copyright © 1998 LinguiSystems, Inc.

Organizational Strategies

❑ time limits for assignments

❑ allowing additional time

❑ highlighting main facts in the book

❑ organizing a notebook or folder

❑ asking student to repeat directions

❑ teaching learning strategies (specify strategy: _____)

❑ repeating directions (e.g., giving written directions as well as verbal)

❑ giving cooperative learning assignments or group assignments

❑ making testing modifications

❑ allowing additional response time during discussions

❑ teaching test-taking skills

Instructional Strategies

❑ giving assignments orally and visually

❑ taping lessons for students

❑ allowing sample or practice tests

❑ providing special materials (specify materials: _____)

❑ providing opportunities for extra drill or skill practice

❑ reducing quantity of material required

❑ requiring better quality of material

❑ modifying oral presentations

❑ providing copies of notes

❑ curriculum compacting

❑ accelerating instruction

❑ providing alternative assignments and tests

❑ using an alternative grading scale

❑ substituting a more appropriate course for a required course

Copyright © 1998 LinguiSystems, Inc.

Bibliography

Bley, Nancy S. and Carol A. Thornton. *Teaching Mathematics to Students with Learning Disabilities, Third Edition.* Austin, TX: Pro-Ed, 1995.

Burns, Marilyn. *Math and Literature (K-3).* Sausalito, CA: Math Solutions Publications, 1992.

Cochran, Judith A. *Reading in the Content Areas for Junior High and High School.* Needham Heights, MA: Allyn and Bacon, 1993.

Core Knowledge Sequence: Grades 1-6. Charlottesville, VA: Core Knowledge Foundation, 1993.

Crawley, Sharon J. and Lee Mountain. *Strategies for Guiding Content Reading: Second Edition.* Needham Heights, MA: Allyn & Bacon, 1995.

English/Language Arts Curriculum Reosurce Handbook: A Practical Guide for K-12 English/Language Arts Curriculum. Millwood, NY: Kraus International Publications, 1992.

Goodman, Yetta and Carolyn Burke. *Reading Strategies: Focus on Comprehension.* New York, Chicago, Dallas: Holt, Rinehart and Winston, 1980.

Gordon, Steven B. and Michael J. Asher. *Meeting the ADD Challenge — A Practical Guide for Teachers.* Champaign, IL: Research Press, 1994.

Hallowell, Edward M., M.D. and John J. Ratey, M.D. *Driven to Distraction, Recognizing and Coping with Attention Deficit Disorder.* New York: Simon & Schuster, 1994.

Hammill Donald D. and Nettie R. Bartel. *Teaching Children with Learning and Behavior Problems – Third Edition.* Boston, MA: Allyn and Bacon, Inc., 1982.

Hillerich, Robert. *Teaching Children to Write, K-8.* Englewood Cliffs, NJ: Prentice-Hall, Inc., 1985.

Lerner, Janet W. *Learning Disabilities: Theories, Diagnosis, and Teaching Strategies, Seventh Edition.* Boston, New York: Houghton Mifflin Company, 1997.

McCarney, Stephen B., Ed.D. *The Attention Deficit Disorders Intervention Manual.* Columbia, MO: Hawthorne Educational Services, Inc., 1989.

Meltzer, Lynn J., Bethany N. Roditi, Donna P. Haynes, Kathleen Rafter Biddle, Michelle Paster, and Susan E. Taber. *Strategies for Success.* Austin, TX: Pro-Ed, 1996.

Osman, Betty and Henriette L. Blinder. *No One to Play With – The Social Side of Learning Disabilities.* Novato, CA: Academic Therapy Publications, 1982.

Powell, Debbie and David Hornsby. *Learning Phonics and Spelling in a Whole Language Classroom.* New York: Scholastic Professional Books, 1993.

Bibliography, continued

Rief, Sandra F. *How to Reach and Teach ADD/ADHD Children.* West Nyack, NY: The Center for Applied Research in Education, 1993.

Sealey, Leonard, Nancy Sealey, and Marcia Millmore. *Children's Writing, An Approach for the Primary Grades.* Newark, DE: International Reading Association, Inc., 1979.

Sorenson, Juanita S., Lynn R. Buckmaster, Mary Kay Francis, and Karen M. Knauf. *The Power of Problem Solving – Practical Ideas and Teaching Strategies for any K-8 Subject Area.* Needham Heights, MA: Allyn and Bacon, 1996.

Thornton, Carol A., Benny F. Tucker, John A. Dossey, and Edna F. Bazik. *Teaching Mathematics to Children with Special Needs.* Menlo Park, CA: Addison-Wesley Publishing Co., 1983.

Whisler, Nancy and Judy Williams. *Literature and Cooperative Learning: Pathway to Literacy.* Sacramento: Literature Co-op, 1990.

Yopp, Ruth Helen and Hallie Kay Yopp. *Literature-Based Reading Activities.* Needham Heights, MA: Allyn and Bacon, 1992.

19-04-14
Copyright © 1998 LinguiSystems, Inc.